# COOKING
## MADE EASY

This edition published in 1994 by SMITHMARK
Publishers Inc., 16 East 32nd Street, New York,
NY 10016.

SMITHMARK books are available for bulk
purchase for sales promotion and premium use.
For details write or call the manager of special
sales, SMITHMARK Publishers Inc., 16 East
32nd Street, New York, NY 10016; (212) 532-
6600.

Food Editors: Rachel Blackmore,
Sheryle Eastwood
Subeditors: Ella Martin, Sheridan Packer
Editorial Coordinator: Margaret Kelly
Recipe Development: Carolyn Fienberg,
Anneka Mitchell

Photography: Ashley MacKevicius,
Andrew Payne
Styling: Wendy Berecry, Rosemary De Santis,
Carolyn Fienberg, Anna Philips

Production Managers: Sheridan Carter,
Nadia Sbisa
Layout and Design: Tara Barrett,
Lulu Dougherty
Finished Art: Chris Hatcher

Some of the contents of this book have been
previously published in other J.B. Fairfax Press
Publications.

JBFP 324 US
Cooking Made Easy
Includes Index
ISBN 0 8317 1227 9

Produced by J.B. Fairfax Press Pty Limited
Printed by Toppan Printing Co, Singapore
PRINTED IN SINGAPORE
10 9 8 7 6 5 4 3 2 1

# COOKING
## MADE EASY

SMITHMARK

# CONTENTS

# Getting started

You will find the recipes in this book are written in an easy-to-follow style, with most ingredients available at your supermarket.

◇ Before you start cooking, look at the recipe and read through the method. Then, following the ingredients listing, collect and prepare all the foods you will require. Use the easy Check-And-Go boxes which appear beside each ingredient; simply check the boxes as you get each item out, then you will have all the ingredients at hand when you start cooking. The ingredients are always listed in their order of use.

◇ The next step is to go through the method and get out the equipment that you will need. You should also consult the recipe at this stage to see if the oven will be used and, if so, turn it on to preheat.

◇ Being organized and assembling all your ingredients and equipment before you start will save you time in cooking and cleaning up.

❖

## BASIC WHITE SAUCE RECIPE

Makes 1 cup (250 mL)

- ☑ **2 tablespoons (30 g) butter**
- ☑ **2 tablespoons all-purpose flour**
- ☑ **¹/₄ teaspoon dry mustard**
- ☑ **1 cup (250 mL) milk**

1  Melt butter in a saucepan; stir in flour and mustard. Cook over medium heat for 1 minute.

2  Remove pan from heat and whisk in milk a little at a time until well blended with butter mixture. Cook over medium heat, stirring constantly until sauce boils and thickens.

**Steaming:** Using this cooking method the food is set over boiling water and cooked in the steam given off. Place the food in a metal basket, on a wire rack, or in a steamer in a saucepan, set ¹/₂-1 inch (1-2.5 cm) above the water. Tightly cover the pan and cook for the required time. Steaming is a popular way of cooking vegetables and fish for the diet conscious. It is one of the best ways to cook food and retain the maximum number of vitamins and minerals.

**Simmering:** This is when liquids are just hot enough for a few bubbles to form slowly and the bubbles burst below the surface. Simmering takes place at a lower temperature than boiling and should not be confused with boiling.

*Remember to collect and measure your ingredients and to get out the equipment you will need before you start cooking*

**Pan cooking:** The food is cooked in a little fat in a skillet. The most commonly used fats are butter, margarine or oil. When pan cooking you need to make sure that the fat is hot enough so that the food cooks without absorbing too much fat, but the fat should not be too hot or the food will burn.

**Boiling:** This is when liquids are hot enough to form bubbles that rise in a steady pattern and break on the surface. The whole mass of liquid starts to move as the bubbling begins.

**Broiling:** Cooking food by direct dry heat. When broiling meat you should place it on a rack in the broiler pan, to allow the fat to drip through. Broiling can be used to cook foods such as steaks, chops and sausages, as well as for browning or toasting the top of denser foods.

**Baking:** Cooking food by indirect dry heat. The food can be cooked covered or uncovered, usually in an oven. Cooking meat in this way is called "roasting".

# Getting equipped

Laminate from Albet Laminati, Equipment from The Bay Tree

Stock Pot

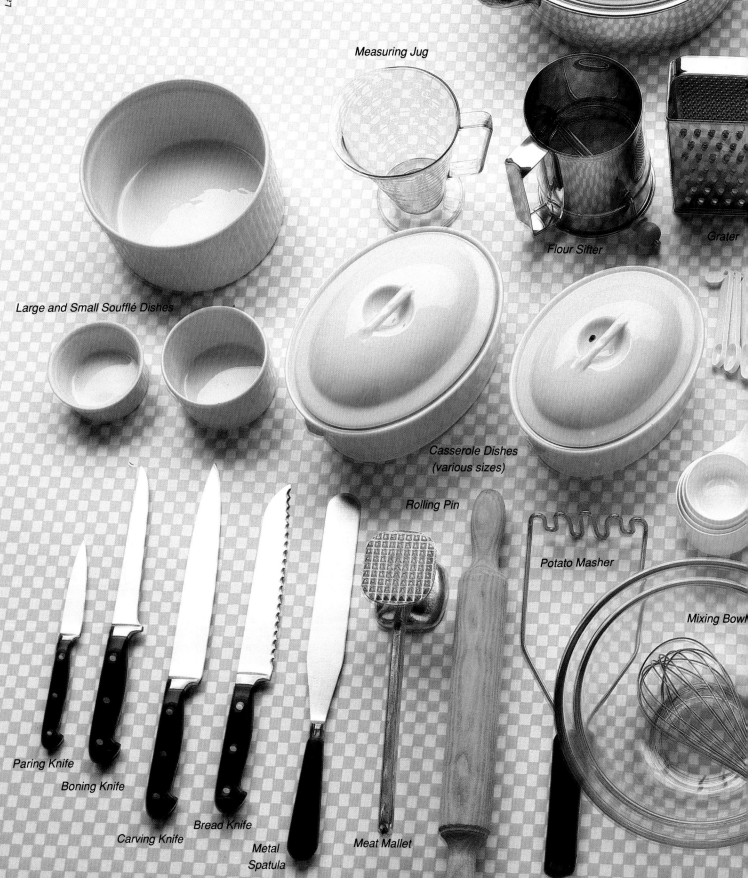

Measuring Jug

Flour Sifter

Grater

Large and Small Soufflé Dishes

Casserole Dishes
(various sizes)

Rolling Pin

Potato Masher

Mixing Bowl

Paring Knife

Boning Knife

Carving Knife

Bread Knife

Metal
Spatula

Meat Mallet

Set of Saucepans

Skillet

Colander

Cake Pans

Wooden Spoon

Cookie Sheet

Pastry Brush

Tongs

easuring Spoons

Rubber Spatula (Rubber Scraper)

easuring Cups

Handheld Electric Beater

Roasting Pan

Wire Whisk

Electric Mixer

# Take an egg

"If there's an egg in the house, there's a meal in the house." When you try these tempting recipes, you will see just how true this is.

❖

## EGGS BENEDICT

*The hollandaise sauce used in this recipe is also great served with poached fish, grilled chicken or steamed vegetables.*

Serves 4

- ☐ **2 teaspoons olive oil**
- ☐ **4 green onions, sliced**
- ☐ **1 green pepper, thinly sliced**
- ☐ **3 slices ham, chopped**
- ☐ **4 eggs**
- ☐ **2 English muffins, split, toasted and buttered**

HOLLANDAISE SAUCE
- ☐ **3 egg yolks**
- ☐ **3 tablespoons water**
- ☐ **$^1/_4$ teaspoon cayenne pepper**
- ☐ **pinch of salt**
- ☐ **$^3/_4$ cup (1$^1/_2$ sticks/180 g) butter, clarified**
- ☐ **1 tablespoon lemon juice**

1   Heat oil in a skillet. Cook green onions and green pepper for 3-4 minutes or until tender. Stir in ham and remove from heat.
2   Break eggs into lightly greased poacher cups. Bring 1 inch (2 cm) of water to the boil, in a skillet large enough to hold the poacher, then lower the heat. Place poacher in pan, cover and simmer for 4-5 minutes or until the whites are firm.
3   To make sauce, place egg yolks, water, cayenne pepper and salt in the top of a double saucepan and whisk until light in color. Cook over low heat and whisk constantly until the mixture thickens. Remove from heat and whisk in butter a little at a time. Stir in lemon juice and set aside for 5 minutes to cool slightly.
4   Top muffins with ham mixture, cooked eggs and sauce.

❖

## MUSHROOM SCRAMBLERS

*A more sophisticated version of scrambled eggs that combines mushrooms, green onions and fresh sage. If you do not have any fresh sage, try using fresh basil, mint or parsley.*

Serves 4

- ☐ **8 eggs**
- ☐ **2 tablespoons milk**
- ☐ **freshly ground black pepper**
- ☐ **2 tablespoons (30 g) butter**
- ☐ **2 oz (50 g) button mushrooms, thinly sliced**
- ☐ **2 green onions, sliced**
- ☐ **2 teaspoons chopped fresh sage**

1   Place eggs and milk in a bowl and, using a whisk, beat to combine. Season to taste with pepper.
2   Melt butter in a medium-size, heavy saucepan. Cook mushrooms, green onions and sage over a medium heat for 2 minutes. Add egg mixture and cook, stirring gently with a wooden spoon, until egg is set but still creamy. Serve immediately.

### RESCUE IT
If hollandaise sauce is overheated, or the butter added too quickly, it will curdle. To rescue curdled sauce, whisk together an egg yolk and 1 tablespoon water in a bowl. Transfer hot hollandaise to a food processor or blender and, with machine running, slowly add egg mixture and process until smooth. Serve immediately.

❖

## SAVORY SCRAMBLERS

*Scrambled eggs are an all-time favorite breakfast or light meal.*

Serves 4

☐ **8 eggs**
☐ **2 tablespoons milk**
☐ **freshly ground black pepper**
☐ **1¹/₂ tablespoons (20 g) butter**

1   Place eggs and milk in a bowl and, using a whisk, beat to combine. Season to taste with pepper.

2   Melt butter in a medium-size, heavy saucepan over low heat. Add egg mixture and cook, stirring gently, until the egg mixture is set but still creamy. Serve immediately.

### Variations

**Herb Scramblers:** Stir 1 teaspoon chopped fresh parsley and 1 teaspoon chopped fresh basil into the egg mixture before cooking.

**Curry Scramblers:** Whisk 1 teaspoon of curry powder into the egg mixture before cooking.

*Mushroom Scramblers, Eggs Benedict, Savory Scramblers*

## EGG AND MUSTARD HAM ROLLS

*In this recipe the eggs are baked in the oven. These rolls make a great snack or a delicious brunch.*

Serves 4

- ☐ **4 wholewheat rolls**
- ☐ **2 tablespoons wholegrain mustard**
- ☐ **1 tablespoon (15 g) butter**
- ☐ **2 oz (50 g) sliced button mushrooms**
- ☐ **1 onion, chopped**
- ☐ **2 oz (50 g) thin slices ham, cut into strips**
- ☐ **freshly ground black pepper**
- ☐ **4 eggs**
- ☐ **$^1/_2$ cup (60 g) shredded Cheddar cheese**

1   Cut a slice from the top of each roll; set aside and reserve. Scoop out the center, leaving a thin shell; reserve crumbs for another use. Spread inside of each roll with mustard.

2   Melt butter in a pan over a medium heat and cook mushrooms and onion for 2-3 minutes. Add ham and cook for 2 minutes longer. Divide the mixture between the rolls and sprinkle with pepper.

3   Break an egg into a small bowl, then slide it into a roll. Repeat with remaining eggs and rolls. Sprinkle with cheese and replace the tops.

4   Place rolls on a cookie sheet and bake at 350°F (180°C) for 25 minutes or until whites are firm.

### Variations

**Egg and Spinach Rolls:** Replace wholegrain mustard with tomato paste, and mushrooms and onion with 6 chopped spinach leaves. Prepare as directed. You may also like to sprinkle the cheese with chopped fresh oregano before baking.

---

### LEFTOVER EGGS

Keep leftover yolks and whites in an airtight container in the refrigerator. Place 1 tablespoon of water over the yolks to prevent a skin from forming. Yolks will keep for up to 3 days and whites for up to 10 days. You can freeze whites for up to one month.

---

### Perfect omelets

✧  If you do not have a special omelet pan, use an aluminum skillet. Prepare the skillet by rubbing with a small amount of salt and paper towel. Remove all traces of salt before cooking. You can also use a nonstick skillet. However, if you intend to make omelets on a regular basis it is well worth investing in a good pan.

✧  For best results the butter should be foaming, but not colored, when you add the egg mixture. This means that the omelet will begin to cook straight away.

### Freshness

The fresher the egg the higher its food value. There are several quick ways to test the freshness of eggs.

✧  When a fresh egg is placed into a glass of water it will sink straight to the bottom.

✧  The yolk of a fresh egg sits in the middle of the egg white when broken onto a saucer.

Note: In case the egg is bad, always break it into a separate glass or container before adding to the main mixture.

## FRENCH OMELET

*For best results, prepare and cook omelets quickly and serve immediately. Remember, if the heat is too high, or the omelet is cooked for too long, it will be tough and dry. Try one of these delicious fillings or make your own favorite combinations.*

Serves 1

- ☐ **2 eggs**
- ☐ **1 tablespoon cold water**
- ☐ **freshly ground black pepper**
- ☐ **1 tablespoon (15 g) butter**

1   Lightly whisk together eggs and water; season to taste with pepper.
2   Heat an omelet pan over a medium heat for 1 minute or until hot. Add butter, tipping the pan so the bottom is completely coated. Heat until the butter is foaming, but not browned, then add the egg mixture. As it sets use a spatula or fork to gently draw up the edge of the omelet until no liquid remains and the omelet is lightly set.
3   Top with filling of your choice and fold in half. Slip omelet onto a plate and serve immediately.

### ❖
## AVOCADO AND BACON FILLING

Serves 1

- ☐ **1 tablespoon sour cream**
- ☐ **1 teaspoon chopped fresh chives**
- ☐ **1/2 teaspoon French mustard**
- ☐ **1 tablespoon chopped bacon**
- ☐ **2 tablespoons chopped avocado**

1   Combine sour cream, chives and mustard. Heat a small skillet and cook bacon until crisp. Remove and drain on paper towels.
2   Spread sour cream mixture over one half of omelet, top with bacon and avocado, fold omelet and serve.

*Above left: Egg and Mustard Ham Rolls, Egg and Spinach Rolls*
*Right: Omelet with Vegetarian Filling, Omelet with Avocado and Bacon Filling*

### ❖
## VEGETARIAN FILLING

Serves 1

- ☐ **1 teaspoon olive oil**
- ☐ **1 tablespoon chopped green pepper**
- ☐ **1 tablespoon finely chopped onion**
- ☐ **1/2 clove garlic, crushed**
- ☐ **1/2 tomato, peeled and chopped**
- ☐ **1 pitted black olive, sliced**
- ☐ **1 teaspoon finely chopped fresh basil**
- ☐ **freshly ground black pepper**

Heat oil in a small saucepan. Cook green pepper, onion and garlic for 2-3 minutes or until onion softens. Add tomato, olive and basil and cook over a medium heat for 5 minutes longer. Season with pepper.

*Boiled eggs*

The way you cook boiled eggs depends on whether you want them soft or hard cooked. Eggs that are at room temperature are less likely to crack during cooking than those taken straight from the refrigerator. The following methods ensure perfect boiled eggs every time.
**Soft cooked:** Bring water to the boil in a saucepan, reduce heat to a simmer and add eggs. Cook for 3 minutes for a light set and 4 1/2 minutes for a slightly firmer set.
**Hard cooked:** Place eggs in cold water, bring to the boil, reduce heat and simmer for 10-12 minutes. Remove eggs and place in a bowl of cold water. Peel eggs as soon as they are cool. This prevents the eggs from becoming tough and a dark ring forming around the yolk.

Pan from The Bay Tree

# Soups and stocks

The basis of a good soup is a full-bodied stock. It is easy to make stock and well worth the little extra time that it takes. Freeze your homemade stock and use as a quick base for soups, casseroles and sauces.

*Spoon from The Bay Tree*

## FRESH TOMATO SOUP

*Bursting with flavor, this satisfying soup makes a great winter luncheon served with crusty bread, or try it chilled on hot summer days. If you find the soup is too tart, a teaspoon of sugar stirred into it will sweeten the flavor.*

Serves 6

- ☐ **1 tablespoon olive oil**
- ☐ **1 carrot, peeled and chopped**
- ☐ **1 onion, chopped**
- ☐ **2 stalks celery, chopped**
- ☐ **1 clove garlic, crushed**
- ☐ **6 tomatoes, peeled, seeded and chopped**
- ☐ **14 oz (440 g) canned tomatoes, drained and chopped**
- ☐ **4 cups (1 litre) chicken stock or broth**
- ☐ **1 teaspoon chopped fresh thyme, or $^1/_4$ teaspoon dried thyme**
- ☐ **$^1/_2$ teaspoon red pepper seasoning**
- ☐ **1 cup (250 mL) cream**
- ☐ **2 tablespoons finely chopped fresh basil**
- ☐ **freshly ground black pepper**

1 Heat oil in a large saucepan, add carrot, onion, celery and garlic and cook for 3-4 minutes or until onion softens.

2 Stir in fresh and canned tomatoes, chicken stock or broth, thyme and red pepper seasoning. Bring to the boil and simmer, uncovered, for 30 minutes. Remove from heat.

3 Place in a food processor or blender and process until smooth. Return soup to pan and bring just to a simmer. Remove from heat and stir in cream and basil. Season to taste with pepper.

---

### CLOUDY CONSOMME?

Consommé should be clear. If your consommé is cloudy it may be because the stock was greasy, unstrained or of poor quality. Whisking the stock after it reaches boiling point or not allowing it to stand before straining will also cause the consommé to become cloudy. Remember that the pan and muslin cloth must be very clean when you are making consommé.

---

## CONSOMME

*Consommé is the French word for a soup based on homemade meat stock that has been enriched, concentrated and then clarified. It is the simplest, yet most sophisticated soup and you may serve it hot or cold. The perfect garnish for consommé is thin strips of blanched carrot and leek.*

Serves 6

- ☐ **4 cups (1 litre) cold beef stock**
- ☐ **8 oz (250 g) ground beef**
- ☐ **1 small onion, chopped**
- ☐ **1 small carrot, chopped**
- ☐ **1 small leek, chopped**
- ☐ **4 whole peppercorns**
- ☐ **bouquet garni**
- ☐ **2 egg whites, lightly beaten**
- ☐ **1 tablespoon dry sherry**

1 Place stock, beef, onion, carrot, leek, peppercorns, bouquet garni and egg whites in a large saucepan, bring slowly to the boil, whisking continuously. Reduce heat, stir in sherry and simmer gently for $1^1/_2$ hours, without stirring.

2 Remove from heat and set aside to stand for 20 minutes. A thick brown scum will have formed on the surface of the stock. Skim off scum and strain carefully through muslin. Remove fat from surface using paper towels.

❖

## CREAM OF MUSHROOM AND HAZELNUT SOUP

*A delightfully creamy soup that makes a great starter for a special occasion. Or, a delicious meal in itself served with crusty French bread and a crispy salad.*

Serves 4

- ☐ $1/4$ **cup ($1/2$ stick/60 g) butter**
- ☐ **3 tablespoons all-purpose flour**
- ☐ **4 cups (1 litre) milk**
- ☐ **2 teaspoons vegetable oil**
- ☐ **6 green onions, chopped**
- ☐ **4 oz (125 g) button mushrooms, sliced**
- ☐ $3/4$ **cup (50 g) hazelnuts (filberts), toasted, skins removed, and finely chopped**
- ☐ **1 teaspoon paprika**
- ☐ $1/2$ **cup (125 mL) cream**
- ☐ **freshly ground black pepper**

1   Melt butter in a medium saucepan. Stir in flour and cook for 1 minute. Remove from heat and gradually stir in milk. Return pan to heat and bring slowly to the boil, stirring constantly. Simmer for 3 minutes, remove from heat and set aside.

2   Heat oil in a medium saucepan and cook green onions for 2 minutes. Add mushrooms, hazelnuts (filberts) and paprika and cook for 2-3 minutes longer. Stir in milk mixture, bring to the boil, then reduce heat and simmer gently for 10 minutes.

3   Remove from heat, place in a food processor or blender and process until smooth. Return soup to a clean pan and reheat gently. Stir in cream and season to taste with pepper.

*Consommé, Fresh Tomato Soup, Cream of Mushroom and Hazelnut Soup*

❖

## HEARTY VEGETABLE SOUP

*This soup is very satisfying as a main meal, or you can serve it in smaller quantities as a starter.*

Serves 6

- ☐ **2 teaspoons (10 g) butter**
- ☐ **2 teaspoons olive oil**
- ☐ **1 onion, finely chopped**
- ☐ **1 clove garlic, crushed**
- ☐ **4 tomatoes, peeled and chopped**
- ☐ **1 potato, peeled and chopped**
- ☐ **1 cucumber, peeled and chopped**
- ☐ **6 cups (1.5 litres) beef stock or broth**
- ☐ **1 cup (125 g) small shell pasta**
- ☐ **1 tablespoon chopped fresh basil**
- ☐ **1 tablespoon chopped fresh parsley**
- ☐ **1 tablespoon lemon juice**
- ☐ **freshly ground black pepper**

1 Heat butter and oil in a large saucepan and cook onion and garlic for 2-3 minutes or until onion softens. Stir in tomatoes, potato and cucumber and cook for 3-4 minutes longer.

2 Add stock or broth, pasta, basil and parsley. Bring to the boil and simmer for 15-20 minutes or until pasta is tender. Stir in lemon juice and season with pepper.

❖

## MEXICAN CORN CHOWDER

*For a less spicy but just as delicious soup you can omit the chili.*

Serves 6

- ☐ **2 teaspoons (10 g) butter**
- ☐ **2 strips bacon, chopped**
- ☐ **1 onion, finely chopped**
- ☐ **2 stalks celery, chopped**
- ☐ **1 small red chili, finely chopped**
- ☐ **2 cups (500 mL) chicken stock or broth**
- ☐ **1 teaspoon ground cumin**
- ☐ **1 teaspoon dried thyme**
- ☐ **2 tablespoons all-purpose flour blended with 3 tablespoons milk**
- ☐ **1³/₄ cups (440 mL) milk**
- ☐ **14 oz (440 g) canned sweet corn kernels, drained**
- ☐ **freshly ground black pepper**

1 Melt butter in a large saucepan and cook bacon, onion, celery and chili for 4-5 minutes or until onion softens.

2 Add stock or broth, cumin and thyme, bring to the boil and simmer for 10 minutes.

3 Stir in flour mixture, then milk and corn kernels, stir continuously until boiling, then reduce heat and simmer for 3 minutes. Season to taste with pepper.

❖

## PEAR AND TARRAGON SOUP

*You can serve this wonderfully flavored fruity soup as a starter, or as a dessert soup. To serve as a dessert, stir in 2 tablespoons honey before processing and replace the tarragon with 2 teaspoons ground nutmeg; omit the pepper.*

Serves 6

- ☐ **2 pounds (1 kg) pears, peeled, cored and chopped**
- ☐ **1 cup (250 mL) water**
- ☐ **³/₄ cup (185 mL) white wine**
- ☐ **2 tablespoons lemon juice**
- ☐ **2 tablespoons lime juice**
- ☐ **2 teaspoons chopped fresh tarragon**
- ☐ **freshly ground white pepper**
- ☐ **¹/₂ cup (125 mL) light cream**

1 Place pears, water, wine, lemon juice, lime juice and tarragon in a large saucepan. Bring to the boil and simmer, uncovered, for 30 minutes.

2 Remove from heat and place in a food processor or blender and process until smooth. Season to taste with pepper and refrigerate until well chilled. Just prior to serving, swirl cream through soup.

❖

## BASIC BEEF STOCK

Makes 8 cups (2 litres)

- ☐ **2 pounds (1 kg) raw beef bones, trimmed of all fat**
- ☐ **8 cups (2 litres) cold water**
- ☐ **6 whole peppercorns**
- ☐ **bouquet garni**
- ☐ **1 onion, chopped**
- ☐ **1 carrot, chopped**
- ☐ **1 leek, chopped**

1 Place bones in a roasting pan and roast, uncovered, at 350°F (180°C) for 30 minutes, or until well browned, turning occasionally.

2 Place bones, water, peppercorns and bouquet garni in a large saucepan. Bring to the boil and simmer gently for 2¹/₂ hours. Skim occasionally during cooking to remove scum. Add onion, carrot and leek and simmer for 1-1¹/₂ hours more. Clarify at end of cooking.

3 Strain stock and cool rapidly. Store and use as required.

❖

## VEGETABLE STOCK

Makes 8 cups (2 litres)

- ☐ **2 large unpeeled yellow onions, quartered**
- ☐ **2 large carrots, roughly chopped**
- ☐ **1 head celery, leaves included, roughly chopped**
- ☐ **1 large bunch parsley, stalks included, roughly chopped**
- ☐ **¹/₂ teaspoon whole black peppercorns**
- ☐ **10 cups (2.5 litres) cold water**

1 Place onions, carrots, celery, parsley, peppercorns and water in a large saucepan. Bring to the boil, reduce heat and simmer for 30 minutes, stirring occasionally.

2 Remove from heat and allow to cool.

3 Purée cold vegetable mixture, then push through a sieve. Refrigerate or freeze until required.

## Making stock

✧ Use fresh meat and vegetables.

✧ Do not use starchy vegetables, such as potatoes, turnips or parsnips as they will produce a cloudy stock. Cauliflower, broccoli or cabbage are too strongly flavored to be used in stocks.

✧ Stocks based on raw bones have the best flavor and make full-bodied, clear stocks that gel on setting.

✧ Use whole black peppercorns for flavor. Ground pepper turns bitter.

✧ Do not season stock with salt. As stock is an ingredient in other recipes it is better to season the finished dish.

✧ Use cold water for making stock.

✧ Using a deep pan will keep evaporation to a minimum.

✧ Long slow simmering makes stock with a full-bodied flavor.

✧ Skim off the scum that rises to the surface during cooking.

✧ Cook fish and seafood stocks for 30 minutes only. A bitter taste can develop if you overcook them.

✧ Skim fat from surface of stock and strain at the end of cooking. Remove fat by dragging strips of paper towels across the surface, or by chilling the stock until the fat solidifies – it can then be lifted off and discarded.

✧ Cool stock before covering. To cool rapidly, place the stock pan in a larger pan of ice cubes and stir.

## Storing stock

✧ You can keep stock in the refrigerator for 3-4 days or in the freezer for up to 12 months.

✧ Even if you are only planning to keep it for a few days, stock keeps better in the freezer.

## Clarifying stock

✧ To clarify stock, add an egg shell or lightly beaten egg white to the stock and simmer for 10 minutes. The scum will be drawn to the surface by the egg shell or white and you can then easily remove it. Strain the stock through a fine sieve lined with several layers of muslin.

✧ Before using muslin, it should first be scalded by pouring boiling water over and through it.

## Note

✧ You can make quick broth soup bases, if desired, from commercial products like canned condensed broth, bouillon cubes or meat concentrates. Simply follow package directions.

*Pear and Tarragon Soup, Hearty Vegetable Soup, Mexican Corn Chowder*

Ladle from The Bay Tree

## CURRIED CHICKEN SOUP

Serves 6

- ☐ ¹/₄ cup (¹/₂ stick/60 g) butter
- ☐ 2 onions, chopped
- ☐ 2 cloves garlic, crushed
- ☐ 2 large parsnips, chopped
- ☐ 4 stalks celery, chopped
- ☐ 3 tablespoons all-purpose flour
- ☐ 1 tablespoon curry powder
- ☐ 6 cups (1.5 liters) chicken stock or broth
- ☐ 6 oz (185 g) frozen green peas
- ☐ 1 pound (500 g) chopped, cooked chicken
- ☐ 1 cup (250 g) sour cream
- ☐ 3 tablespoons finely chopped fresh flat-leaf parsley
- ☐ 2 tablespoons chopped fresh dill weed

1   Melt butter in a large saucepan, cook onions, garlic, parsnips and celery for 5-6 minutes. Stir in flour and curry powder and cook for 1 minute longer.

2   Remove pan from heat and gradually blend in stock or broth. Cook over a medium heat, stirring constantly, until mixture boils and thickens. Reduce heat, stir in peas and chicken and cook for 10 minutes.

3   Remove pan from heat and whisk in sour cream, then stir in parsley and dill weed. Cook over a low heat, stirring frequently, for 3-4 minutes or until warmed through. Serve immediately.

## PEA AND SALAMI SOUP

*Variations of this soup have been around since the Middle Ages. This one with salami is perfect for a fireside supper.*

Serves 6

- ☐ 1¹/₂ pounds (750 g) dried split peas, rinsed
- ☐ 16 cups (4 liters) water
- ☐ 1 pound (500 g) bacon bones
- ☐ 4 onions, finely chopped
- ☐ 4 tablespoons chopped celery leaves
- ☐ 4 stalks celery, chopped
- ☐ 8 oz (250 g) salami, cut into ¹/₂-inch (1 cm) cubes
- ☐ freshly ground black pepper

1   Place split peas and water in a large heavy saucepan and set aside to let stand overnight.

2   Add bacon bones to pan with peas. Bring to a boil, then reduce heat and simmer for 2 hours or until soup thickens. Stir in onions, celery leaves and celery and cook over a low heat for 20 minutes longer.

3   Remove bacon bones from soup and discard. Add salami and cook until heated through. Season to taste with pepper.

❖

## POTATO BACON CHOWDER

Serves 6

- ☐ 8 oz (250 g) bacon, chopped
- ☐ 2 tablespoons (30 g) butter
- ☐ 2 large onions, chopped
- ☐ 4 stalks celery, chopped
- ☐ 2 teaspoons dried thyme
- ☐ 2 tablespoons all-purpose flour
- ☐ 6 cups (1.5 liters) chicken stock or broth
- ☐ 2 large potatoes, peeled and cubed
- ☐ 1¼ cups (315 g) sour cream
- ☐ 3 tablespoons chopped fresh parsley
- ☐ 2 tablespoons snipped fresh chives

1   Place bacon in a large saucepan and cook over a medium heat for 5 minutes or until golden and crisp. Remove bacon from pan and drain on paper towels.

2   Melt butter in pan and cook onions, celery and thyme over a low heat for 4-5 minutes or until onions are soft.

3   Return bacon to pan, then stir in flour and cook for 1 minute. Remove pan from heat and gradually blend in stock or broth. Return pan to heat and bring to a boil, then reduce heat. Add potatoes and cook for 10 minutes or until potatoes are tender.

4   Remove pan from heat and stir in sour cream and parsley. Return pan to heat and cook without boiling, stirring constantly, for 1-2 minutes. Sprinkle with chives and serve immediately.

*Left: Curried Chicken Soup, Pea and Salami Soup*
*Right: Potato Bacon Chowder*

# Take some mince

Ground beef provides value-for-money meals. A little goes a long way and can be stretched even further by adding soft bread crumbs or vegetables. It can be made into balls, patties, burgers and loaves.

❖

## BASIC MEATLOAF

*Serve this meatloaf hot with vegetables as a main meal, or cold cut into slices for sandwiches. Try one of the tasty toppings below to change the flavor completely.*

Serves 4

- ☐ **1 pound (500 g) lean ground beef**
- ☐ **1 cup (60 g) soft bread crumbs**
- ☐ **3 tablespoons beef stock or broth**
- ☐ **1 onion, grated**
- ☐ **1 carrot, shredded**
- ☐ **2 eggs, lightly beaten**
- ☐ **1 teaspoon dried mixed herbs**
- ☐ **1 teaspoon Worcestershire sauce**
- ☐ **freshly ground black pepper**

1   Place meat, bread crumbs, stock or broth, onion, carrot, eggs, mixed herbs and sauce in a bowl. Season to taste with pepper and mix well to combine.
2   Press mixture into a lightly greased 5 x 8-inch (13 x 20 cm) ovenproof loaf pan and bake at 350°F (180°C) for 40-45 minutes. Drain off any liquid, cover and allow to stand for 10 minutes before turning out and serving.

❖

## TEX-MEX TOPPING

- ☐ **¹/₂ cup (125 mL) catsup**
- ☐ **1 tablespoon bottled barbecue sauce**
- ☐ **1 teaspoon brown sugar**
- ☐ **1 teaspoon chili sauce**
- ☐ **2 tablespoons finely chopped green pepper**
- ☐ **1 oz (25 g) packet corn chips, crushed**
- ☐ **¹/₂ cup (60 g) shredded Cheddar cheese**

Combine catsup, barbecue sauce, brown sugar, chili sauce and green pepper. Turn meatloaf onto an ovenproof plate. Spread Tex-Mex Topping over surface of meatloaf. Top with corn chips and cheese and bake at 400°F (200°C) for 10 minutes or until cheese melts.

❖

## HONEY-GLAZED TOPPING

- ☐ **¹/₄ cup (30 g) pepitas (Mexican pumpkin seeds)**
- ☐ **¹/₄ cup (30 g) sunflower seeds**
- ☐ **2 tablespoons pine nuts**
- ☐ **2 tablespoons honey**
- ☐ **1 tablespoon brown sugar**
- ☐ **2 tablespoons lemon juice**
- ☐ **¹/₂ teaspoon dry mustard**

1   Combine pepitas, sunflower seeds and pine nuts. Turn meatloaf onto an ovenproof plate and spread top with seed mixture.
2   Place honey, brown sugar, lemon juice and mustard in a saucepan and heat until honey melts and all ingredients are blended. Pour mixture over meatloaf and bake at 400°F (200°C) for 10 minutes.

❖

## INDIVIDUAL PASTRY-WRAPPED MEATLOAVES

Serves 4

- ☐ **1 recipe Basic Meatloaf**
- ☐ **4 sheets prepared puff pastry, thawed**
- ☐ **1 egg, lightly beaten**

1   Make up Basic Meatloaf mixture and divide into four equal portions. Press one portion of meat mixture down the center of each pastry sheet to form a rectangle.
2   Brush edges of pastry with egg and wrap up like a parcel. Decorate top with leaves cut from pastry scraps. Place rolls on a greased roasting rack in a baking dish. Brush pastry with egg and bake at 350°F (180°C) for 25-30 minutes, or until pastry is golden and crisp.

*Basic Meatloaf with Tex-Mex Topping, Individual Pastry-Wrapped Meatloaves, Chili Con Carne, Melting Meatballs*

Spoon from Bibelot

❖

## MELTING MEATBALLS

Serves 4

- ☐ **1 recipe Basic Meatloaf**
- ☐ **3 oz (90 g) Cheddar cheese, cut into twelve $^1/_2$-inch (1.5 cm) cubes**
- ☐ **1 cup (45 g) unprocessed bran**
- ☐ **3 tablespoons finely chopped pistachio nuts**
- ☐ **all-purpose flour**
- ☐ **1 egg, lightly beaten**
- ☐ **oil for cooking**

1  Divide meatloaf mixture into twelve equal portions. Wrap one portion of meat around each cheese cube, to make a ball. Repeat with remaining meat and cheese.
2  Combine bran and pistachio nuts. Coat meatballs in flour, dip in egg and roll in bran mixture.
3  Heat oil in a skillet and cook meatballs, turning occasionally, for 6-8 minutes or until golden brown and cooked through.

❖

## CHILI CON CARNE

Serves 4

- ☐ **1 tablespoon polyunsaturated oil**
- ☐ **1 onion, chopped**
- ☐ **2 cloves garlic, crushed**
- ☐ **3 small red chilies, finely chopped**
- ☐ **1 pound (500 g) lean ground beef**
- ☐ **$^1/_4$ teaspoon ground cloves**
- ☐ **$^1/_2$ teaspoon ground cumin**
- ☐ **1 teaspoon dried oregano leaves**
- ☐ **2 teaspoons paprika**
- ☐ **14 oz (440 g) canned tomatoes, undrained and mashed**
- ☐ **1 tablespoon tomato paste**
- ☐ **$^1/_2$ cup (125 mL) beef stock or broth**
- ☐ **10 oz (310 g) canned red kidney beans, drained and rinsed**
- ☐ **freshly ground black pepper**

1  Heat oil in a skillet; cook onion, garlic and chili for 2-3 minutes or until onion softens.
2  Stir in ground beef, cloves, cumin, oregano and paprika. Cook for 5-6 minutes or until meat browns. Combine tomatoes, tomato paste and stock or broth and pour into pan. Reduce heat and simmer for 20 minutes or until liquid reduces by half.
3  Add kidney beans and cook for 10 minutes longer, or until heated through. Season to taste with pepper.

# Take a piece of steak

Steak is wonderfully versatile. Don't waste the more expensive cuts in the long cooking processes such as stewing; they will lose juices and become tough.

## BEEF WITH PAPRIKA AND WINE RAGOUT

Serves 4

- [ ] **2 tablespoons olive oil**
- [ ] **1¹/₂ pounds (750 g) chuck steak, cut into 1-inch (2.5 cm) cubes**
- [ ] **2 large onions, chopped**
- [ ] **2 cloves garlic, crushed**
- [ ] **1 tablespoon (15 g) butter**
- [ ] **1 tablespoon all-purpose flour**
- [ ] **2 tablespoons paprika**
- [ ] **14 oz (440 g) canned tomatoes, undrained and mashed**
- [ ] **¹/₂ cup (125 mL) red wine**
- [ ] **¹/₂ cup (125 mL) beef stock or broth**
- [ ] **freshly ground black pepper**
- [ ] **¹/₂ cup (125 g) sour cream or plain yogurt (optional)**

1   Heat oil in a large saucepan; cook meat cubes a few at a time, until color changes. Remove from pan and set aside. Continue browning remaining meat.

2   Add onions to the pan and cook for 4-5 minutes or until golden. Stir in garlic and cook for 1 minute longer. Remove from pan and set aside.

3   Melt butter in the same pan, blend in flour and paprika and cook over a medium heat for 1 minute. Combine tomatoes, wine and stock or broth. Pour into pan. Cook over medium heat until mixture boils and thickens. Reduce heat. Return meat and onion mixture to the pan. Season to taste with pepper. Cover and simmer for 2 hours, stirring occasionally.

4   Remove pan from heat and just prior to serving stir in sour cream to give a creamed, marbled effect.

### Variation

**Easy Beef Curry:** Omit paprika and replace with curry powder. Omit wine and during the last 30 minutes of cooking add 3 tablespoons chopped dried apricots, 1 tablespoon seedless raisins and 1 tablespoon fruit chutney. Replace the sour cream with coconut milk.

## BEEF WITH SWEET AND SOUR SAUCE

Serves 4

- [ ] **2 tablespoons oil**
- [ ] **1 pound (500 g) lean round steak, cut into thin strips**
- [ ] **1 onion, cut into eighths**
- [ ] **2 cloves garlic, crushed**
- [ ] **1 teaspoon grated fresh ginger**
- [ ] **4 oz (100 g) oyster mushrooms, sliced**
- [ ] **2 stalks celery, sliced diagonally**
- [ ] **2 carrots, sliced diagonally**
- [ ] **¹/₂ red pepper, chopped**
- [ ] **¹/₂ green pepper, chopped**
- [ ] **14 oz (440 g) canned baby corn, drained**
- [ ] **4 oz (100 g) snow peas, trimmed**

SAUCE

- [ ] **2 teaspoons chili sauce**
- [ ] **2 tablespoons vinegar**
- [ ] **2 tablespoons catsup**
- [ ] **2 tablespoons brown sugar**
- [ ] **2 tablespoons dry sherry**
- [ ] **1 tablespoon cornstarch, blended with ¹/₂ cup (125 mL) pineapple juice**

1   Heat oil in a skillet or wok. Stir-fry meat for 2-3 minutes or until it changes color. Remove meat from the pan and set aside.

2   Add onion, garlic and ginger to the pan and stir-fry for 1 minute. Stir in mushrooms, celery, carrots, red and green peppers, corn and snow peas. Stir-fry for 2-3 minutes. Remove from pan and set aside.

3   To make sauce, combine chili sauce, vinegar, catsup, brown sugar, sherry and cornstarch mixture. Pour into pan and cook for 1 minute or until mixture boils and thickens. Return meat and vegetables to the pan. Stir-fry for 1-2 minutes or until heated through.

## BEEF WITH SATAY SAUCE

Serves 6

- ☐ 1½ pounds (750 g) lean sirloin or round steak

MARINADE
- ☐ **2 tablespoons light soy sauce**
- ☐ **2 teaspoons cornstarch**
- ☐ **2 tablespoons honey**
- ☐ **1 teaspoon grated fresh ginger**
- ☐ **1 clove garlic, crushed**
- ☐ **1 teaspoon grated lemon rind**
- ☐ **1 tablespoon dry sherry**

SATAY SAUCE
- ☐ **½ cup (125 g) peanut butter**
- ☐ **3 tablespoons finely chopped, unsalted peanuts**
- ☐ **¾ cup (185 mL) chicken stock or broth**
- ☐ **4 tablespoons dry white wine**
- ☐ **1 tablespoon soy sauce**
- ☐ **1 teaspoon grated lemon rind**
- ☐ **1 teaspoon grated fresh ginger**
- ☐ **1 clove garlic, crushed**
- ☐ **1 teaspoon chili sauce**
- ☐ **½ teaspoon curry paste (vindaloo)**

1  Trim meat of all visible fat, cut into 1-inch (2.5 cm) cubes and thread onto twelve oiled bamboo skewers.
2  To make marinade, combine soy sauce, cornstarch, honey, ginger, garlic, lemon rind and sherry in a glass bowl. Add meat and set aside to marinate.
3  To make sauce, place peanut butter, peanuts, stock or broth, wine, soy sauce, lemon rind, ginger, garlic, chili sauce and curry paste in a saucepan. Cook over a low heat for 2-3 minutes or until heated through and all ingredients are well blended.
4  Remove skewers from marinade and broil meat for 5-6 minutes, turning and basting with marinade frequently during cooking. Serve with satay sauce.

---

## THE PERFECT STEAK

Everyone has their own preference on how they like their steak cooked; steak can be cooked to rare, medium-rare and well-done. Rare meat is springy to touch, medium meat less springy and well-done has very little give in it. When testing, press with blunt tongs. Do not pierce or cut the meat with a knife as this causes loss of juices and dryness.

---

## STEAK WITH A DEVILED MARINADE

Serves 4

- ☐ **4 boneless rib-eye steaks (Delmonico)**

MARINADE
- ☐ **1 teaspoon curry powder**
- ☐ **2 tablespoons brown sugar**
- ☐ **2 tablespoons catsup**
- ☐ **2 teaspoons Worcestershire sauce**
- ☐ **1 teaspoon soy sauce**
- ☐ **2 teaspoons lime juice**

1  Trim meat of all visible fat and set aside.
2  To make marinade, combine curry powder, sugar, catsup, Worcestershire sauce, soy sauce and lime juice in a glass bowl. Add meat and set aside to marinate for 2-4 hours.
3  Remove meat from marinade, broil on medium-high heat for 3-4 minutes each side. Baste frequently with marinade during cooking.

---

*Meaty matters*

**Marinating:** This is a clever way of tenderizing and adding flavor to less tender cuts of meat. To make a basic marinade you require oil; flavorings, such as herbs and spices; and an acid ingredient, such as wine, soy sauce, lemon juice or a wine vinegar, to break down tough meat fibers. Place the meat and marinade in a bowl, cover and store in the refrigerator until required. The quantity of marinade should be just sufficient to form a pool to coat the meat. Turn the meat occasionally during marinating to ensure all sides come in contact with the marinade.

**Stir-frying:** This is a very quick method of cooking. The meat is usually cut into strips, across the grain, to ensure quick even cooking. For best results, cook meat in batches of no more than 1 pound (500 g). Use a medium-high heat and move the meat back and forth in the pan constantly for 2-3 minutes or until it just changes color. The addition of vegetables adds flavor, texture and nutrients, making this type of meal one that all the family will look forward to.

---

## MEAT TENDERNESS

Use only the less tender cuts of meat, such as chuck, flank or blade, for making ragouts. These cuts are from the more active part of the animal, so are made up of more fibers and connective tissue, therefore require slow, moist cooking for tenderness.

---

*From left: Steak with a Deviled Marinade, Beef with Paprika and Wine Ragout, Beef with Satay Sauce, Beef with Sweet and Sour Sauce*

# Dinner for two

This menu will serve two people. For four servings, the meat quantity will remain the same, but you will need to double the quantities of the vegetable dishes.

## Setting a table

The most exciting part of having a dinner party is creating an atmosphere. The table can be compared to a stage, where the food and setting inspire the mood for the occasion. The setting can also allow your personal artistic ability to flourish. The choice of dinnerware and cutlery will depend on your menu, however, there are a few logical rules you should remember.

*Glasses from Villeroy and Boch*

✧ When you are laying out the cutlery it is usual to place forks to the left of the setting with spoons and knives to the right; the cutting edge of the knives should face inwards. You should arrange the cutlery in the order in which it is to be used, working from the outside, in towards the dinnerware. It is acceptable, and often easier, to have no more than three pieces of cutlery at either side and to place dessert spoons and forks on the table after the main course.

✧ Arrange glasses at the top right-hand corner of each place setting, in the opposite order of use to the cutlery. Working from the inside out, start with the sherry glasses through to champagne flutes.

✧ Color, where possible, should coordinate – food, china and table coverings. Your food should be fresh and bright, attractively and simply arranged, giving thought to texture, taste and color.

❖

## GARLIC POTATO AND CARROT CAKES

Serves 2

☐ **1 large potato**
☐ **1 small carrot, shredded**
☐ **1 egg, lightly beaten**
☐ **2 tablespoons (30 g) butter**
☐ **1 clove garlic, crushed**

1   Boil, steam or microwave potato until partially cooked. Drain and refresh under cold running water. Peel and shred coarsely into a bowl. Add carrot and egg and toss lightly. Season to taste.
2   Divide mixture into four equal portions, shape into rounds and flatten slightly. Melt butter in a skillet and cook garlic for 1 minute. Add potato cakes and cook until golden brown, turning once.

❖

## HONEYED SWEET POTATO AND BEET

Serves 2

☐ **1 large raw beet, peeled and cut into $^1/_2$-inch-wide (1 cm) strips**
☐ **1 small sweet potato, peeled and cut into $^1/_2$-inch-wide (1 cm) strips**
☐ **2 tablespoons (30 g) butter**
☐ **1 teaspoon grated orange rind**
☐ **2 tablespoons orange juice**
☐ **2 teaspoons Grand Marnier**
☐ **1 tablespoon honey**

1   Boil, steam or microwave beet and sweet potato separately until just tender. Drain and refresh under cold running water. Set aside.
2   Melt butter in a skillet, stir in orange rind, orange juice, Grand Marnier and honey. Cook over medium heat until honey melts and all ingredients are well blended.
3   Toss in beet and sweet potato and cook until heated through. Serve immediately.

---

### LEFTOVER ROASTS

Cut any leftover beef into slices, place on a plate, spoon over your favorite sauce, cover and reheat in the microwave oven on MEDIUM (50%) for 3-4 minutes or until heated through. Or fill pita bread with cold slices of beef tossed with your favorite salad ingredients. Grind leftovers in the food processor and add to some cooked onions, with flavorings of your choice. Thicken and spoon into an ovenproof dish. Top with a layer of mashed potato and a sprinkling of shredded Cheddar cheese. Bake at 400°F (200°C) for 15-20 minutes or until golden.

❖

## ROASTED BEEF WITH HORSERADISH SAUCE

Serves 2

☐ **1 pound (500 g) beef tenderloin, in one piece**
☐ **freshly ground black pepper**
☐ **2 tablespoons (30 g) butter**
☐ **3 tablespoons brandy**

HORSERADISH SAUCE
☐ **$^1/_2$ cup (125 mL) mayonnaise**
☐ **$^1/_2$ cup (125 mL) plain yogurt**
☐ **1 teaspoon lemon juice**
☐ **1 teaspoon bottled horseradish relish**
☐ **1 avocado, peeled, pitted and chopped**

1   Trim all visible fat from meat and sprinkle with pepper. Tie with string at even intervals to retain the shape during cooking. Heat butter over medium-high heat in a baking dish and sear meat on all sides until golden brown. Spoon brandy over meat and bake at 350°F (180°C) for 20-25 minutes or until cooked as desired, basting frequently with pan juices.
2   To make sauce combine mayonnaise, yogurt, lemon juice, horseradish and avocado in a food processor or blender. Process until smooth. Slice beef and serve with sauce.

*Left: Setting a table*
*Right: Roasted Beef with Horseradish Sauce, Honeyed Sweet Potato and Beet, Garlic Potato and Carrot Cakes*

**MENU IDEA**
Serve this main course accompanied by half the quantity of Pear and Tarragon Soup (page 16) as a first course and follow the main course with half the quantity of Nut Bavarian Cream (page 83).

# Roasting

Roasting was originally done over an open fire where very large pieces of meat were turned over glowing embers until cooked through. As culinary skills improved so did roasting methods.

## STEP–BY–STEP ROASTING

1  Preheat oven to 325°-350°F (170°-180°C).
2  Trim excess fat and weigh meat to calculate cooking time.
3  Refer to Quick Roasting Guide below for cooking times.
4  After the cooking time is completed, remove meat from the oven and cover with aluminum foil and set aside to stand for 10-15 minutes. Standing allows the juices to settle and makes carving easier.

### Roasting notes

**Lamb:** Irrespective of the weight, lamb rib loin, rack or crown roast is only cooked for a total of 40-55 minutes at 400°F (200°C).
**Pork:** Pork is always cooked to well-done as in the Quick Roasting Guide.

### Keeping it hot

One of the most daunting tasks when serving a hot meal is actually managing to get it to the table hot. If you follow these easy tips your meals will be hot every time.

✧  Start by heating the plates.

✧  You can heat plates by placing them in a warm oven for 10-15 minutes; some ovens contain warming drawers in which plates can be heated.

✧  Plates can also be heated by placing in a sink of very hot water for a few minutes. You need to dry them thoroughly before using.

✧  Have all the food ready before you start serving.

✧  You will find that some foods retain their heat longer than others; for example, whole or large portions of vegetables stay hot longer than slices of meat and smaller cut vegetables, so serve these first.

✧  If your oven size permits, the plates with food on can be returned to the oven, set at 350°F (180°C) and kept warm for up to 10 minutes. Be careful not to overheat as this causes the food to lose moisture and to look unappetizing.

✧  Sauces or gravy are best placed in a sauce jug and each person allowed to serve themselves.

## ROASTING IT

There are several methods of roasting. The method you choose will depend on the cut of meat you wish to roast.

**Dry heat roasting:** The meat is first seared to seal in the juices and moisture, then oven-baked at a high temperature for a short period. This way of roasting is ideal for those who enjoy meat browned on the outside and rare in the center. The more tender cuts of meat, such as beef loin, boneless sirloin, boneless rib and veal loin should be used for this method.
**French roasting:** The meat is cooked over a bed of chopped vegetables with stock or broth or wine and covered for most of the cooking. The cover is removed towards the end of cooking to brown the meat. Rib roasts, round tip and boneless briskets are the most suitable cuts for this method.
**Pot roasting:** The more economical cuts of meat that would be tough if dry roasted are used for this method. The meat is first seared over a medium-high heat to seal in the juices, then transferred to a covered roasting dish (Dutch oven) and cooked slowly in the oven, or simmered in a covered, large, deep heavy-based saucepan on top of the stove. In both cases the lid must fit tightly. A small quantity of liquid and vegetables can be added if desired and basting is not required. Suitable cuts to use are round, brisket, rolled thick flank, blade-bone and chuck.

## ROASTING CUTS
Suitable cuts for roasting are –
**Beef:** Loin, Rib, Sirloin, Chuck, Blade, Brisket, Flank, Round Tip or Rump
**Veal:** Boneless Shoulder Roast, Rib, Loin, Sirloin, Rump, Breast
**Lamb:** Shoulder, Cushion, Rib, Crown, Loin, Leg, Sirloin
**Pork:** Blade Boston, Arm Picnic, Rib, Crown, Loin, Sirloin, Tenderloin, Hocks Ham

| QUICK ROASTING GUIDE | | |
|---|---|---|
| | COOKING TIME (per 1 pound/500 g) | INTERNAL TEMPERATURE |
| RARE | 20-25 minutes | 140°F (60°C) |
| MEDIUM | 25-30 minutes | 160°F (70°C) |
| WELL-DONE | 30-35 minutes | 170°F (75°C) |

# Veal

Veal is a very lean, tender, fine-grained meat that cooks quickly. Take care not to overcook veal or it will become tough and dry.

❖

## VEAL CASSEROLE WITH A CHEESE COBBLER TOPPING

Serves 4

- ☐ **4 medium veal arm or blade steaks, cut into 2-inch (5 cm) pieces**
- ☐ **all-purpose flour**
- ☐ **2 tablespoons olive oil**

SAUCE
- ☐ **4 oz (125 g) mushrooms, sliced**
- ☐ **1 clove garlic, crushed**
- ☐ **3 green onions, chopped**
- ☐ **1 teaspoon French mustard**
- ☐ **1¼ cups (310 mL) chicken stock or broth**
- ☐ **freshly ground black pepper**
- ☐ **2 teaspoons cornstarch blended with ½ cup (125 mL) cream or evaporated skim milk**

CHEESE COBBLER TOPPING
- ☐ **2 cups (250 g) self-rising flour**
- ☐ **pinch cayenne pepper**
- ☐ **pinch chili powder**
- ☐ **½ cup (1 stick/125 g) butter**
- ☐ **1 egg, lightly beaten**
- ☐ **½ cup (125 mL) milk**
- ☐ **¾ cup (90 g) shredded Cheddar cheese**
- ☐ **½ teaspoon dry mustard**

1   Trim meat of all visible fat and toss in flour. Heat oil in a skillet and cook meat until brown. Transfer to a shallow baking dish.
2   To make sauce, add mushrooms, garlic and green onions to the pan. Cook until mushrooms are soft and place on top of meat. Combine mustard and stock or broth, pour into the pan and bring to the boil; season to taste with pepper. Whisk in cornstarch mixture and cook over medium heat, stirring, until sauce boils and thickens. Spoon over meat and vegetables. Cover and bake at 350°F (180°C) for 40 minutes.

3   To make topping, sift flour, cayenne and chili powder into a large mixing bowl. Cut in 6 tablespoons (90 g) butter until mixture resembles fine bread crumbs. Combine egg and milk and pour into flour mixture all at once. Stir ingredients together to give a soft, sticky dough. Turn mixture out onto a floured surface and knead lightly. Roll out dough to ½-inch (1 cm) thickness and cut into rounds with a 2-inch (5 cm) cutter.
4   Remove baking dish from oven, uncover and, working quickly, top with biscuit rounds. Melt remaining butter and combine with cheese and mustard. Spread over biscuits and bake at 425°F (220°C) for 12-15 minutes, or until golden brown.

*Left: Glazed Minted Lamb Racks with Roast Vegetables (page 30)*
*Right: Veal Casserole with a Cheese Cobbler Topping*

*Casserole Dish from The Bay Tree*

# Take a schnitzel

When you are pan-cooking, veal needs to be protected against moisture loss and dryness. You can do this by coating it with a flour and crumb mixture.

## CRISPY COATINGS

Coatings protect the meat during cooking, and add texture and flavor. You might like to try ground nuts, crushed corn flakes, crushed chips, rolled oats, bran, sesame seeds and packaged stuffings. You will require flour, egg and your choice of coating ingredient.

**Flour:** All-purpose flour is used and can be seasoned with any powdered flavoring, such as paprika or curry powder. Use flour sparingly: a guideline is $^1/_4$ cup (30 g) of flour to 8 oz (250 g) of meat. The easiest way to apply flour, is to place the flour and seasonings in a freezer bag. Pat the meat dry with paper towels and place in the bag, one piece at a time. Shake the bag until the meat is completely coated with flour, then remove meat from bag, shaking off excess flour.

**The egg:** Food is dipped into egg to provide a surface for the coating to stick to. Egg is a high protein food which coagulates when it comes in contact with heat, forming a moisture-proof barrier around the food and enclosing the natural juices. The egg is lightly beaten and usually diluted with a tablespoon of milk. The diluted mixture adheres more readily to the food.

**The coating:** This is pressed onto the egg-dipped food until the entire surface is covered. You can store any leftover coating in an airtight container for use at a later date. You might like to add herbs and grated cheese for extra flavor.

❖

## TROPICAL BANANA AND COCONUT SCHNITZEL

Serves 4

- ☐ 4 boneless veal cutlets (approximately 5 oz/155 g each)
- ☐ oil for cooking

COATING
- ☐ 2 eggs, lightly beaten
- ☐ 2 large bananas, mashed
- ☐ $^1/_2$ teaspoon ground allspice
- ☐ $^1/_2$ cup (70 g) macadamia nuts, finely chopped
- ☐ 4 tablespoons shredded coconut
- ☐ 1 cup (30 g) crushed corn flakes
- ☐ all-purpose flour

SPICY BROWN SAUCE
- ☐ $^1/_2$ cup (125 g) crunchy peanut butter
- ☐ 3 teaspoons brown sugar
- ☐ 1 tablespoon Benedictine liqueur
- ☐ 1 cup (250 mL) water
- ☐ 1 clove garlic, crushed
- ☐ 1 teaspoon grated fresh ginger
- ☐ 2 teaspoons curry powder
- ☐ 1 teaspoon chili sauce or to taste
- ☐ 2 tablespoons cream

1 Place cutlets between two sheets of wax paper. Pound meat lightly with a mallet to $^1/_4$-inch (5 mm) thickness. Cut small slits around edges to prevent curling.
2 To make coating, combine egg, banana and allspice and set aside. Mix together nuts, coconut and corn flakes. Coat meat with flour, dip in banana mixture and coat with nut mixture. Refrigerate for 30 minutes.
3 To make sauce, place peanut butter, sugar, Benedictine, water, garlic, ginger, curry powder and chili sauce in a saucepan and heat through over a low heat. Remove from heat and stir in cream.
4 Heat oil in a skillet. Cook veal for 3-4 minutes each side, or until golden brown. Remove from pan and drain on paper towels. Spoon sauce over and serve immediately.

❖

## CHEESY SCHNITZELS WITH GINGERED CITRUS SAUCE

Serves 4

- ☐ 4 boneless veal cutlets (approximately 5 oz/155 g each)
- ☐ oil for cooking

*Tropical Banana and Coconut Schnitzel, Cheesy Schnitzels with Gingered Citrus Sauce, Veal and Avocado Rolls*

## COATING

- ☐ **1 cup (125 g) crushed cheese-flavored crackers**
- ☐ **2 teaspoons dried chives**
- ☐ **2 teaspoons dried onion flakes**
- ☐ **all-purpose flour**
- ☐ **1 egg, lightly beaten**

## GINGERED CITRUS SAUCE

- ☐ **1¼ cups (300 mL) thick cream or evaporated skim milk**
- ☐ **1 tablespoon ginger wine**
- ☐ **2 tablespoons dry white wine**
- ☐ **1 teaspoon grated orange rind**
- ☐ **1 teaspoon grated lime rind**
- ☐ **1 tablespoon lime juice**
- ☐ **1 tablespoon orange juice**
- ☐ **1 tablespoon finely chopped preserved ginger in syrup**
- ☐ **2 egg yolks, lightly beaten**

1  Place cutlets between two sheets of wax paper. Pound meat lightly with a mallet to ¼-inch (5 mm) thickness. Cut small slits around edges to prevent curling.

2  To make coating, combine crushed crackers, chives and onion flakes. Coat meat with flour, dip in egg and coat with cracker mixture.

3  Heat oil in a skillet, cook veal cutlets two at a time, over a medium heat for 3-4 minutes each side, or until golden brown. Set aside and keep warm. Drain oil from pan and wipe clean with paper towels.

4  To make sauce, place cream, ginger wine, wine, orange rind, lime rind, lime juice, orange juice and ginger in pan. Bring to the boil, then reduce heat and simmer uncovered for 10 minutes. Remove from heat and whisk in egg yolks. Stir over a low heat until sauce thickens. Place meat on a serving plate, spoon sauce over and serve.

❖

# VEAL AND AVOCADO ROLLS

Serves 4

- ☐ **4 large boneless veal cutlets**
- ☐ **oil for cooking**

## STUFFING

- ☐ **2 tablespoons (30 g) butter**
- ☐ **1 leek, finely sliced**
- ☐ **1 tablespoon chopped fresh basil**
- ☐ **1 teaspoon finely chopped fresh rosemary**
- ☐ **1 teaspoon grated lemon rind**
- ☐ **1 avocado, peeled, pitted and finely chopped**
- ☐ **1 cup (60 g) soft bread crumbs**

## COATING

- ☐ **1 tablespoon sesame seed**
- ☐ **1 teaspoon grated lemon rind**
- ☐ **1 cup (125 g) dry bread crumbs**
- ☐ **all-purpose flour**
- ☐ **3 eggs, lightly beaten**

## PORT WINE SAUCE

- ☐ **½ cup (125 mL) chicken stock or broth**
- ☐ **3 tablespoons port wine**
- ☐ **2 teaspoons cornstarch blended with 3 tablespoons cream**

1  Place cutlets between two sheets of wax paper. Pound meat lightly with a mallet to ¼-inch (5 mm) thickness. Cut each cutlet in half across the grain.

2  To make stuffing, melt butter in a skillet. Cook leek for 2-3 minutes or until soft. Remove pan from heat and stir in basil, rosemary, lemon rind, avocado and bread crumbs. Spread a heaped spoonful over each piece of meat. Roll up and secure with wooden picks.

3  To make coating, combine sesame seeds, lemon rind and bread crumbs. Coat rolls with flour, dip into egg and roll in bread crumb mixture. Repeat egg and bread crumb steps. Refrigerate for 30 minutes.

4  Heat oil in a skillet. Cook rolls a few at a time until golden brown and cooked through. Remove from pan and drain on paper towels. Set aside and keep warm.

5  To make sauce, drain oil from pan. Add stock or broth and bring to the boil. Reduce heat and stir in port and cornstarch mixture. Cook over a medium heat until sauce boils and thickens. Spoon sauce over rolls and serve.

*Coat meat with flour, then dip in egg mixture and finally in coating*

# Lamb

Lamb is one of the most versatile of meats. Almost all the cuts are prime, and therefore suitable for dry roasting, pan-cooking and broiling. Lamb should be bright in color, fresh in appearance with a lean cover of pale cream fat.

❖

## GLAZED MINTED LAMB RACKS

Serves 4

- ☐ **2 lean lamb cutlets, each containing 6 rib bones**

CRACKED WHEAT SEASONING
- ☐ **4 tablespoons cracked wheat (bulgur)**
- ☐ **1/2 cup (30 g) soft bread crumbs**
- ☐ **3 tablespoons finely chopped fresh parsley**
- ☐ **1 tablespoon finely chopped fresh mint**
- ☐ **1 teaspoon grated lemon rind**
- ☐ **1 tablespoon pine nuts, toasted**
- ☐ **2 teaspoons mint jelly**
- ☐ **1 apple, peeled, cored and shredded**
- ☐ **1 tablespoon (15 g) butter, melted**
- ☐ **freshly ground black pepper**

MINT GLAZE
- ☐ **3 tablespoons mint jelly**
- ☐ **2 tablespoons orange juice**
- ☐ **2 tablespoons honey**

1   Using a sharp knife, separate bones from meat, leaving both ends intact. (This makes a pocket for the seasoning.) Trim excess fat from outside of ribs.
2   To make seasoning, cover cracked wheat with boiling water and set aside to stand for 15 minutes. Drain and rinse under cold running water. Dry on paper towels and place in a mixing bowl with bread crumbs, parsley, mint, lemon rind, pine nuts, mint jelly, apple, butter, and pepper to taste. Pack mixture firmly into pockets. Place racks in a roasting pan.
3   To make glaze, place mint jelly in a saucepan and cook over a medium heat until melted. Stir in orange juice and honey. Brush racks with glaze and bake at 375°F (180°C) for 30-35 minutes or until cooked to individual taste. Baste frequently with glaze during cooking.

❖

## ROAST VEGETABLES

Serves 4

- ☐ **4 potatoes, peeled and halved**
- ☐ **4 pieces butternut squash, peeled**
- ☐ **4 yellow onions, peeled**
- ☐ **1 tablespoon polyunsaturated oil**

1   Boil or steam potatoes for 5 minutes. Drain and dry on paper towels. Set aside until cool enough to handle. Score the upper rounded side of potatoes with a fork. This helps to crisp potatoes during cooking.
2   Brush potatoes, squash and onions with oil and place in roasting pan and bake at 375°F (180°C) for about 1 hour or until golden and crisp. Remove from pan and keep warm.

❖

## GRAVY FROM PAN JUICES

Makes 1 1/2 cups (375 mL)

- ☐ **1 1/2 tablespoons all-purpose flour**
- ☐ **1 1/2 cups (375 mL) beef stock or broth**
- ☐ **1 teaspoon Worcestershire sauce**

1   Drain all but 2 tablespoons of fat from roasting pan. Place pan over heat, stir in flour and cook over a medium heat until lightly browned.
2   Remove pan from heat and gradually blend in stock or broth and Worcestershire sauce. Return to heat and cook, stirring constantly until gravy boils and thickens. Strain gravy into a small saucepan and cover to prevent a skin forming. Reheat when required.

*Glazed Minted Lamb Racks with Roast Vegetables*

## Meaty matters

**Buying meat:** The first and most important rule to follow when buying meat is to get to know your butcher. After all, the butcher is the best person to advise you on what cuts are most suitable for your cooking needs. If you do have a bad experience with poor quality meat, don't be afraid to mention this when you are next in the store. It could be that you used the wrong cooking method for the cut of meat.

✧ When selecting meat, look for meat with a clear, but not too bright color. Avoid meat with a greyish tinge and dried edges.

**Storing meat:** Meat should be unpacked, loosely wrapped in plastic food wrap and stored in the refrigerator or freezer as soon as possible after purchasing.

✧ If it is not frozen, ground meat and thin cuts of veal should be eaten within a day or two of buying.

✧ Chops, steaks and cubed pieces can be left for two to three days in the refrigerator.

✧ Roasts will keep, refrigerated, for up to one week.

**Microwaving meat:** While some meat meals are ideal for microwave cooking others require a little care.

✧ Roasting meat in the microwave oven is simple, if you remember a few rules.

✧ The less tender cuts such as chuck or brisket, which are usually made into stews and casseroles, should be cooked on a lower power setting.

✧ Your roast will cook more evenly if you elevate it on a microwave-safe roasting rack.

✧ If using a meat thermometer to register the internal temperature of meat, insert into thickest part of the roast, avoiding any fat or bone. Do not use a conventional meat thermometer in the microwave oven; it must be one that is designed specifically for microwave use.

✧ The edges of the meat will cook first. To prevent these from overcooking, shield edges and high points with strips of aluminum foil when they are cooked. You should make sure that foil does not touch the walls of the microwave oven.

✧ On completion of cooking allow standing time. The internal temperature of the meat will rise slightly, completing the cooking.

✧ Wrap the meat in aluminum foil and stand the meat for 10-15 minutes.

✧ Standing time also allows the juices in the meat to settle, making carving easier.

✧ When cooking racks of lamb or crown roasts, shield the bones with aluminum foil throughout the cooking.

31

## LAMB AND VEGETABLE FILO PARCELS

Serves 4

- ☐ 8 lean lamb rib chops
- ☐ 2 cloves garlic, cut into slivers
- ☐ 2 teaspoons wholegrain mustard
- ☐ 3 oz (90 g) blue cheese
- ☐ 1 tablespoon (15 g) butter, softened
- ☐ 1 teaspoon port wine
- ☐ 16 sheets filo pastry
- ☐ 3 tablespoons olive oil

VEGETABLE FILLING
- ☐ 1 tablespoon (15 g) butter
- ☐ 4 green onions, chopped
- ☐ 1 red pepper, finely chopped
- ☐ 8 button mushrooms, chopped
- ☐ 2 large lettuce leaves, finely shredded

1   Trim meat of all visible fat and insert a sliver of garlic between meat and bone of each chop. Broil chops each side on medium heat until just browned but not cooked through. Spread both sides of chops with mustard. Combine blue cheese, butter and port. Top each chop with a spoonful of cheese mixture.

2   To make vegetable filling, melt butter in a skillet and cook green onions, pepper, mushrooms and lettuce for 2-3 minutes or until onions soften and lettuce wilts. Set aside to cool slightly.

3   Working with 2 sheets of pastry, brush between sheets with oil, fold in half, then in half again to form a square. Brush between folds with oil. Spread a little of the vegetable mixture over pastry, top with a chop, then top with more vegetable mixture. Fold pastry to enclose chop, leaving bone exposed, brush with oil and place on a cookie sheet.

4   Repeat with remaining pastry, chops and vegetable mixture. Bake at 425°F (220°C) for 10 minutes or until golden brown.

## LAMB WITH RED CURRANT SAUCE

Serves 4

- ☐ 4 large, lean, lamb blade or arm chops

RED CURRANT SAUCE
- ☐ 1 tablespoon lime juice
- ☐ ¹/₂ cup (125 g) red currant jelly
- ☐ 2 tablespoons French mustard

1   Trim excess fat from chops. Broil, pan cook or barbecue for 4-5 minutes each side or until cooked to individual liking. Set aside and keep warm.

2   To make sauce, place lime juice, red currant jelly and mustard in a small saucepan and cook gently until jelly melts and all ingredients are blended. Spoon sauce over chops and serve.

## LAMB AND WINTER VEGETABLE HOTPOT

Serves 4

- ☐ 2 tablespoons polyunsaturated oil
- ☐ 8 lean, lamb blade or arm chops, meat cut into 1-inch (2.5 cm) cubes
- ☐ 1 large onion, quartered
- ☐ 1 large carrot, thickly sliced
- ☐ 2 stalks celery, sliced
- ☐ 1 parsnip, sliced
- ☐ 1 small turnip, diced
- ☐ 1 potato, diced
- ☐ ¹/₄ cup (¹/₂ stick/60 g) butter
- ☐ 4 tablespoons all-purpose flour freshly ground black pepper
- ☐ 1 tablespoon finely chopped fresh thyme
- ☐ 1 tablespoon finely chopped fresh rosemary
- ☐ 2 cups (500 mL) chicken stock or broth
- ☐ 1 tablespoon Worcestershire sauce
- ☐ 2 teaspoons soy sauce
- ☐ 2 tablespoons catsup
- ☐ 1 cup (125 g) frozen peas

1   Heat oil in a large saucepan and cook meat in batches until brown on all sides. Remove from pan and set aside. Add onion to the pan and cook for 2-3 minutes, or until golden. Stir in carrot, celery, parsnip, turnip and potato. Reduce heat to low, cover and cook vegetables for 5 minutes, stirring occasionally. Remove from pan and set aside.

2   Drain oil from pan and wipe clean. Melt butter in same pan. Stir in flour, pepper, thyme and rosemary and cook for 4-5 minutes, or until flour is a light straw color.

Remove pan from heat. Blend in stock or broth, Worcestershire, soy and catsup sauces. Cook over a medium heat, stirring frequently until sauce boils and thickens.
3 Return meat and vegetables to the pan. Cover and simmer gently for 1½ hours or until meat is tender.

---

### COOK'S TIP

Noisettes (English chops) are rolled, boneless loin double chops. The meat is rolled up tightly and tied. Most butchers are happy to prepare noisettes for you if you order them in advance.

---

❖

## LAMB WITH A TANGY APRICOT SAUCE

Serves 4

- ☐ **8 lamb noisettes (English chops)**

TANGY APRICOT SAUCE
- ☐ **½ cup (125 g) apricot jam**
- ☐ **1 tablespoon soy sauce**
- ☐ **1 clove garlic, crushed**
- ☐ **½ teaspoon ground cinnamon**
- ☐ **1 tablespoon white wine vinegar**

1 Grill, pan cook or barbecue noisettes for 4-5 minutes each side or until cooked to desired liking. Set aside and keep warm.
2 To make sauce, place jam, soy sauce, garlic, cinnamon and vinegar in a small saucepan. Cook gently over a low heat until jam melts and all ingredients are blended. Spoon sauce over noisettes.

---

❖

## CRUSTY INDIVIDUAL LAMB AND KIDNEY PIES

Serves 4

FILLING
- ☐ **1½-pounds (750 g) boneless lamb shoulder**
- ☐ **3 lamb kidneys**
- ☐ **¼ cup (½ stick/60 g) butter**
- ☐ **1 onion, chopped**
- ☐ **4 strips bacon, chopped**
- ☐ **2 tablespoons all-purpose flour**
- ☐ **3 tablespoons red wine**
- ☐ **¾ cup (185 mL) chicken stock or broth**
- ☐ **1 tablespoon tomato paste**
- ☐ **½ teaspoon sugar**
- ☐ **1 tablespoon finely chopped fresh thyme**
- ☐ **freshly ground black pepper**

CRUST
- ☐ **½ cup ( 1 stick/125 g) butter, softened**
- ☐ **2 cups (300 g) sour cream**
- ☐ **1 egg**
- ☐ **1½ cups (185 g) self-rising flour**
- ☐ **1 tablespoon finely chopped fresh parsley**

1 Remove all visible fat from lamb. Cut into 1-inch (2.5 cm) cubes. Trim kidneys of visible fat and soak in salted water for 10 minutes. Wipe dry with paper towels. Slash the skin on the rounded side of each kidney and draw it back on each side until it is attached by the core only. Draw out as much core as possible and cut, with skin, close to the kidney. Cut each kidney into slices.

2 Melt 2 tablespoons (30 g) butter in a large saucepan. Cook meat in batches until browned on all sides. Remove from pan and set aside. Add kidney to the pan and cook for 1-2 minutes or until just sealed. Remove from pan and set aside. Stir in onion and bacon and cook for 2-3 minutes or until golden. Remove from pan and set aside.
3 Melt remaining butter. Add flour and cook for 3-4 minutes or until a light straw color. Blend in wine, stock or broth, tomato paste and sugar and cook over medium heat, stirring constantly until sauce boils and thickens. Season with thyme and pepper. Return meat mixture to the pan, cover and simmer gently for 1½ hours or until meat is tender. Set aside to cool slightly.
4 To make crust, combine butter, sour cream and egg in a bowl. Sift in 1 cup (125 g) of flour and add parsley. Mix until well combined. Divide two-thirds of mixture into four equal portions. Press each portion over bottom and sides of four individual dishes, and spoon in filling. Lightly knead remaining flour into the remaining dough. Press out on a lightly floured surface, using palm of hand, to ½-inch (1 cm) thickness and cut into rounds using a 1¼-inch (3 cm) metal pastry cutter. Top filling with dough rounds, overlapping them slightly. Bake at 350°F (180°C) for 30 minutes, or until golden brown.

*From left: Lamb with a Tangy Apricot Sauce, Lamb with Red Currant Sauce, Lamb and Winter Vegetable Hotpot, Crusty Individual Lamb and Kidney Pies, Lamb and Vegetable Filo Parcels*

# *Take some pork*

Succulent pork is still one of the most popular meats. Pork should be cooked just long enough to retain its moisture and texture. If you overcook it the texture and flavor will deteriorate.

❖

## ROASTED PORK LOIN

Serves 8

- ☐ **3 pounds (1$^1$/2 kg) boneless rolled pork center loin roast**

SEASONING
- ☐ **2 tablespoons (30 g) butter**
- ☐ **4 spinach leaves, stalks removed and leaves shredded**
- ☐ **3 tablespoons pine nuts**
- ☐ **$^1$/2 cup (30 g) soft bread crumbs**
- ☐ **$^1$/4 teaspoon ground nutmeg**
- ☐ **freshly ground black pepper**

CHUNKY APPLE AND PEAR SAUCE
- ☐ **1 small green apple, peeled, cored and sliced**
- ☐ **1 small pear, peeled, cored and sliced**
- ☐ **2 teaspoons chopped dried dates**
- ☐ **4 tablespoons apple juice**
- ☐ **2 teaspoons honey**
- ☐ **1 teaspoon grated lemon rind**
- ☐ **pinch ground cloves**

1   Unroll loin and make a cut in the middle of the fleshy part of the meat, making a space for the seasoning.
2   To make seasoning, melt butter in a skillet. Cook spinach and pine nuts for 2-3 minutes or until spinach wilts. Remove pan from heat and stir in bread crumbs, nutmeg, and pepper to taste. Spread spinach mixture over cut flap.
3   Roll up loin firmly and secure with string. Place in a rack in roasting pan. Bake at 350°F (180°C) for 1$^1$/2 hours or until juices run clear when pierced with a skewer or meat thermometer registers 170°F (77°C).
4   To make sauce, place apple, pear, dates, apple juice, honey, lemon rind and cloves in a small saucepan. Cover and bring to the boil. Reduce heat and simmer for 5 minutes, or until apple is tender.

❖

## HONEY-GLAZED PORK

Serves 4

- ☐ **1 pound (500 g) pork tenderloin, in one piece**

GLAZE
- ☐ **1 tablespoon honey**
- ☐ **1 tablespoon orange juice**
- ☐ **1 teaspoon light soy sauce**

Trim meat of all visible fat and connective tissue. Place in a roasting pan. Combine honey, orange juice and soy sauce and brush over pork. Bake at 350°F (180°C) for 30 minutes. Halfway through cooking turn and brush with any leftover glaze. Slice pork, spoon over sauce of your choice, and serve.

❖

## BANANA AND APRICOT SAUCE

- ☐ **1 banana, chopped**
- ☐ **1 teaspoon lemon juice**
- ☐ **14 oz (440 g) canned apricot halves**
- ☐ **$^1$/4 teaspoon ground cinnamon**
- ☐ **2 tablespoons coconut cream**

1   Place banana, lemon juice, undrained apricots, cinnamon and coconut cream in a food processor or blender and process until smooth.
2   Transfer to a small saucepan and cook gently without boiling, until heated through.

---

### BUYING PORK

When you buy pork it should be pale-fleshed with a sweet smell, not slimy or bloody. The good news is that pork is now being bred much leaner making it ideal for today's lifestyle.

---

*Pork cuts*

**Loin of pork:** A loin of pork makes a great smaller roast. You can specify the size by the number of chops you require and so avoid waste. Don't be afraid to ask your butcher to remove the bones for a boneless loin. You might like to pack a boneless loin with a fruit or savory filling.

**Butterfly pork steaks:** These steaks are basically thick rib chops, boned, cut almost in half and opened out flat. Try placing a fruit or savory filling on one side of the steak, then folding it over and securing with wooden picks. This is just like making stuffed pork chops only without the bones. You can then pan cook or bake these steaks.

**Pork tenderloin:** Pork tenderloin is a lean piece of meat taken from the loin ribs. Tenderloin is quick and easy to cook and there is no waste. You can roast or pan cook pork tenderloin, then serve sliced, with a sauce.

❖

## MUSTARD SAUCE

Serves 4

- ☐ **2 tablespoons (30 g) butter**
- ☐ **1$^1$/2 tablespoons all-purpose flour**
- ☐ **2 teaspoons Dijon-style mustard**
- ☐ **$^3$/4 cup (190 mL) chicken stock or broth**
- ☐ **1 teaspoon lime juice**
- ☐ **freshly ground black pepper**
- ☐ **3 tablespoons mayonnaise**

1   Melt butter in a saucepan, stir in flour and mustard and cook for 1 minute. Remove pan from heat and blend in stock or broth and lime juice. Season to taste.
2   Cook over a medium heat, stirring frequently until sauce boils and thickens. Remove from heat and stir in mayonnaise.

❖

## TOMATO SAUCE WITH APPLE

Serves 4

- ☐ **1 tomato, peeled, seeded and chopped**
- ☐ **1 small apple, peeled, cored and grated**
- ☐ **2 tablespoons orange juice**
- ☐ **1 tablespoon tomato paste**
- ☐ **1$^1$/2 tablespoons apricot jam**
- ☐ **$^1$/4 teaspoon yellow mustard seeds**

Place tomato, apple, orange juice, tomato paste, jam and mustard seeds in a saucepan. Cook over medium heat, stirring frequently until sauce boils and all ingredients are well blended.

# PORK WITH CABBAGE AND CARAWAY SEEDS

*Ask your butcher to prepare butterfly pork steaks from thick rib chops as described on previous page.*

Serves 4

- ☐ **4 large, lean, pork butterfly steaks**
- ☐ **1 tablespoon (15 g) butter**

FILLING

- ☐ **2 cups savoy cabbage, finely shredded**
- ☐ **1 stalk celery, finely sliced**
- ☐ **$^1/_2$ cup (90 g) cooked white rice**
- ☐ **1 teaspoon caraway seeds**
- ☐ **2 tablespoons sour cream or plain yogurt**
- ☐ **freshly ground black pepper**

SAUCE

- ☐ **2 tablespoons brown sugar**
- ☐ **2 tablespoons (30 g) butter**
- ☐ **3 tablespoons dry white wine**
- ☐ **$^1/_2$ cup (125 mL) chicken stock or broth**
- ☐ **3 tablespoons cider vinegar**
- ☐ **$^1/_2$ teaspoon cornstarch blended with 1 teaspoon of water**

1 Trim meat of all visible fat. Place each steak between two sheets of plastic food wrap and pound lightly with a rolling pin.

2 To make filling, boil, steam or microwave cabbage and celery, separately, until just tender. Drain and refresh under cold running water. Dry between sheets of paper towels.

3 Combine cabbage, celery, rice, caraway seeds, sour cream and pepper to taste. Divide mixture between steaks and spread over one half of each steak. Fold steaks over and secure with wooden picks. Melt butter in a skillet and cook steaks on both sides until golden brown. Place steaks in a baking dish and set aside. Wipe pan clean.

4 To make sauce, place sugar and butter in a pan and cook until sugar dissolves. Blend in wine, stock or broth and vinegar and simmer for 3 minutes. Pour over steaks in baking dish. Bake uncovered at 350°F (180°C) for 20-30 minutes or until tender. Baste with sauce frequently during cooking.

5 Strain sauce from pan and place in a small saucepan. Stir in cornstarch mixture and heat until sauce thickens slightly. Spoon over steaks and serve.

*Top: Roasted Pork Loin*
*Center: Honey-Glazed Pork with Banana and Apricot Sauce, Mustard Sauce, Tomato Sauce*
*Bottom: Pork with Cabbage and Caraway Seeds*

Plate from Villeroy and Boch

Plate from Studio HAUS

Plate from Powder Blue

35

# Chicken

Childhood memories include roast chicken with a tasty stuffing. Today's busy homemaker can buy chicken cut into the right pieces for the recipe – drumsticks, thighs, breasts.

❖

## CHICKEN DRUMSTICK CASSEROLE

Serves 4

- [ ] 8 chicken drumsticks
- [ ] $1/2$ cup (60 g) all-purpose flour
- [ ] 3 tablespoons olive oil
- [ ] 1 onion, sliced
- [ ] 1 clove garlic, crushed
- [ ] 2 tablespoons (30 g) butter
- [ ] 1 cup (250 mL) dry red wine
- [ ] $1/2$ cup (125 mL) chicken stock or broth
- [ ] 14 oz (440 g) canned tomatoes, undrained and mashed
- [ ] 2 teaspoons finely chopped fresh rosemary
- [ ] 8 oz (250 g) button mushrooms, halved
- [ ] 3 tablespoons cream
- [ ] freshly ground black pepper

1 Coat drumsticks with 4 tablespoons of flour. Heat 2 tablespoons olive oil in a large skillet, add drumsticks and brown. Remove from pan and set aside.
2 Add onion and garlic to pan and cook for 3-4 minutes or until onion softens. Add butter and melt. Stir in remaining flour and cook for 1 minute. Return chicken to pan.
3 Combine wine, stock or broth, tomatoes and rosemary and add to pan. Bring to the boil and simmer for 30 minutes, or until drumsticks are cooked through.
4 Heat remaining oil in a small skillet and cook mushrooms for 3-4 minutes. Stir mushrooms and cream into chicken mixture. Season to taste with pepper.

### COOK'S TIP
You may wish to use a variety of chicken pieces, such as wings or thighs, with the drumsticks. If you are watching your weight, remove the skin from the chicken before cooking. Most of the fat in the chicken is found in the skin.

### IS YOUR BIRD COOKED?
✧ To test when a bird is cooked place a skewer into the thickest part of the breast and when the skewer is removed the juices should run clear. If the juices are tinged pink return bird to the oven and continue cooking.
✧ On completion of cooking allow whole birds to stand for 10-20 minutes. This tenderizes the meat by allowing the juices to settle into the flesh.

❖

## FETA DRUMSTICKS

Serves 6

- [ ] 2 tablespoons (30 g) butter
- [ ] 1 clove garlic, crushed
- [ ] 1 bunch English spinach, finely shredded
- [ ] 2 slices ham, finely chopped
- [ ] $1/2$ cup (125 g) feta cheese, broken into small pieces
- [ ] 1 teaspoon ground coriander
- [ ] 3 teaspoons ground nutmeg
- [ ] freshly ground black pepper
- [ ] 12 chicken drumsticks
- [ ] 2 tablespoons olive oil

1 Melt butter in a skillet, add garlic and cook for 1 minute. Stir in half the spinach and cook for 3-4 minutes, or until spinach is tender. Remove from pan and set aside. Repeat with remaining spinach.
2 Combine spinach mixture, ham, cheese, coriander and 1 teaspoon nutmeg. Season to taste with pepper. Ease skin carefully away from drumstick to form a pocket. Place a spoonful of mixture into the pocket and pull skin over. Repeat with remaining mixture and drumsticks.
3 Brush drumsticks with oil, sprinkle with remaining nutmeg and place in a baking dish. Bake at 350°F (180°C) for 30 minutes, or until drumsticks are cooked through.

Bowl from Lifestyle Imports

## TAKE A STUFFING

A stuffing transforms succulent roast chicken into something extra special. For a change, instead of placing the stuffing in the cavity of the bird try placing it between the skin and the flesh.

## BASIC BREAD STUFFING

- ☐ **2 cups (125 g) soft bread crumbs**
- ☐ **1 onion, finely chopped**
- ☐ **$^1/_4$ cup ($^1/_2$ stick/60 g) butter, melted**
- ☐ **1 egg, lightly beaten**
- ☐ **$^1/_3$ cup (85 g) pine nuts, toasted**
- ☐ **2 teaspoons chopped fresh parsley**
- ☐ **1 tablespoon chopped fresh rosemary**
- ☐ **freshly ground black pepper**

Combine bread crumbs, onion, butter, egg, pine nuts, parsley and rosemary in a bowl and mix well. Season to taste with freshly ground black pepper and use as desired.

### Variations

**Fruity Stuffing:** Soak $^3/_4$-cup (125 g) chopped mixed fruit in $^1/_2$ cup (125 mL) of dry white wine for 30 minutes. Mix into the basic stuffing. Fruits such as apricots, prunes and currants are popular choices. Replace the rosemary with 1 teaspoon of mixed spice.

**Ham and Mushroom Stuffing:** Add to the basic stuffing 1 cup (125 g) finely chopped ham, $^1/_2$ cup (90 g) sliced button mushrooms that have been cooked in 1 teaspoon of olive oil, and 1 tablespoon French mustard.

**Hot 'n' Spicy Stuffing:** Add $^1/_2$ teaspoon chili powder to the basic stuffing. Replace pine nuts with the same quantity of sunflower seeds and replace parsley and rosemary with 1 teaspoon ground cumin and 1 teaspoon garam masala.

*Feta Drumsticks, Chicken Drumstick Casserole*

## ROAST CHICKEN AND CURRIED RICE STUFFING

Serves 4

- ☐ 3 pounds (1.5 kg) chicken
- ☐ 4 slices bacon, chopped
- ☐ 4 green onions, chopped
- ☐ 2 teaspoons curry powder
- ☐ 2¹/₂ cups (440 g) cooked long grain rice
- ☐ 1 cup (60 g) soft bread crumbs
- ☐ 1 tablespoon olive oil

TOMATO AND MUSHROOM SAUCE
- ☐ 2 tablespoons (30 g) butter
- ☐ 1 onion, chopped
- ☐ 1 green pepper, chopped
- ☐ 4 oz (125 g) mushrooms, sliced
- ☐ 14 oz (440 g) canned tomatoes, undrained and mashed
- ☐ 2 tablespoons tomato paste
- ☐ 3 tablespoons red wine
- ☐ 1 tablespoon sugar
- ☐ ¹/₂ cup (125 mL) water
- ☐ freshly ground black pepper

1 Wash chicken and pat dry with paper towels. Cook bacon, green onions and curry powder in a skillet until bacon is crisp. Remove from heat and stir in rice and bread crumbs.

2 Fill chicken with rice mixture, securing opening with a skewer. Place in a baking dish, brush with oil and bake at 350°F (180°C) for 1¹/₂ hours, basting frequently with pan juices.

3 To make sauce, melt butter in a saucepan and cook onion, green pepper and mushrooms for 2-3 minutes. Stir in tomatoes, tomato paste, wine, sugar and water. Cook over medium heat, stirring occasionally, for 8-10 minutes or until sauce has reduced by a quarter. Season to taste with pepper. Serve sauce with chicken.

## CITRUS CHICKEN SALAD

*A great dish for picnics or outdoor eating.*

Serves 4

- ☐ 12 oz (375 g) cooked skinned, boned chicken, cut into strips
- ☐ 8 oz (250 g) cooked vegeroni noodles, drained, rinsed and cooled
- ☐ 4 green onions, chopped
- ☐ 1 orange, peeled and flesh chopped
- ☐ 1 bunch curly endive, leaves separated and washed
- ☐ 3 tablespoons orange juice
- ☐ 1 teaspoon soy sauce
- ☐ freshly ground black pepper

1 Combine chicken, noodles, green onions and orange. Line a salad bowl with endive and add chicken mixture.

2 Combine orange juice and soy sauce. Pour over salad and toss to coat ingredients. Season to taste with pepper. Cover and refrigerate until ready to serve.

## ORANGE CHICKEN

Serves 4

- ☐ 4 boned, skinned chicken breast halves
- ☐ 2 teaspoons cornstarch blended with 3 tablespoons chicken stock or broth

MARINADE
- ☐ ³/₄ cup (185 mL) orange juice
- ☐ 1 tablespoon finely grated orange rind
- ☐ ¹/₂ teaspoon French mustard
- ☐ ¹/₂ teaspoon ground nutmeg
- ☐ ¹/₂ teaspoon curry powder
- ☐ freshly ground black pepper

1 To make marinade, combine orange juice, orange rind, mustard, nutmeg and curry powder in a shallow glass dish. Season to taste with pepper. Add chicken, cover and marinate for 1-2 hours.

2 Transfer chicken and a little of the marinade to a baking dish and bake at 350°F (180°C) for 30 minutes or until chicken is tender. Place remaining marinade and cornstarch mixture in a saucepan. Cook over a medium heat, stirring constantly, until sauce boils and thickens. Spoon sauce over chicken and serve.

## CHICKEN DONER KABOBS

*These homemade kabobs are sure to be a winner with friends and family.*

Serves 4

- ☐ 3 tablespoons (45 g) butter
- ☐ 4 boned, skinned chicken breast halves, cut into thin strips
- ☐ 2 teaspoons curry powder
- ☐ ¹/₂ teaspoon sweet chili sauce
- ☐ 2 tablespoons tomato sauce
- ☐ 1 small bunch watercress
- ☐ 1 red onion, sliced
- ☐ 1 tomato, sliced
- ☐ 4 large rounds pita bread, warmed

1 Melt butter in a small skillet and stir-fry chicken for 3 minutes or until color changes. Stir in curry powder, chili sauce and tomato sauce and cook for 1 minute.

2 Layer chicken, watercress, onion and tomato over pita bread and roll up to enclose filling. Serve immediately.

## APRICOT CHICKEN BURGERS

Serves 4

- ☐ 1¹/₂ tablespoons plain yogurt or mayonnaise
- ☐ 2 tablespoons snipped fresh chives
- ☐ 4 plain or wholewheat hamburger buns, split
- ☐ 1 small ripe avocado, pitted, peeled and sliced
- ☐ 1 mignonette lettuce, leaves separated and shredded

CHICKEN BURGERS
- ☐ 8 oz (250 g) lean ground chicken
- ☐ 1 egg, lightly beaten
- ☐ 5 dried apricots, finely chopped
- ☐ 1 small carrot, shredded
- ☐ 1 small zucchini, shredded
- ☐ 30 g (1 oz) shredded Cheddar cheese

1 Combine yogurt or mayonnaise and chives. Split buns and spread with yogurt or mayonnaise mixture. Set aside.

2 To make burgers, combine ground chicken, egg, apricots, carrot, zucchini and cheese in a bowl. Divide mixture into four equal portions and shape each portion into a pattie. Cook patties in a nonstick skillet for 6-7 minutes each side, or until golden.

3 To assemble burgers, place cooked patties on base of prepared buns, then top with avocado, lettuce and top of bun.

*Roast Chicken and Curried Rice Stuffing*

# Take a chicken fillet

## STRAWBERRY CHICKEN WITH PINK PEPPERCORN SAUCE

*Delicately different, this chicken breast holds a fruity surprise and is accompanied by a subtle pepper sauce.*

Serves 4

- ☐ **4 boned, skinned chicken breast halves**
- ☐ **¹/₄ cup (30 g) finely chopped almonds**
- ☐ **1 cup (125 g) strawberries, hulled and chopped**

SAUCE
- ☐ **2 tablespoons (30 g) butter**
- ☐ **1 tablespoon all-purpose flour**
- ☐ **4 tablespoons red wine**
- ☐ **4 tablespoons milk**
- ☐ **¹/₂ cup (125 mL) cream**
- ☐ **¹/₂ teaspoon mixed spice**
- ☐ **1 tablespoon pink peppercorns, rinsed and drained**
- ☐ **freshly ground black pepper**

1   Remove all visible fat from chicken. Place halves between two pieces of plastic food wrap and pound with a rolling pin to flatten.
2   Sprinkle each half with almonds and strawberries. Fold in shorter ends and then roll up to enclose the filling. Secure with wooden picks. Place on a rack in a roasting pan and bake at 350°F (180°C) for 15-20 minutes or until chicken is cooked through.
3   To make sauce, melt butter in a small saucepan, stir in flour and cook for 1 minute. Remove from heat.
4   Combine wine, milk, cream and mixed spice and gradually stir into flour mixture. Cook over medium heat, stirring constantly, until sauce thickens slightly. Remove from heat and add peppercorns. Season to taste with pepper and serve with chicken rolls.

*Chicken with Almonds and Herbs, Cheesy Chicken Rolls, Strawberry Chicken with Pink Peppercorn Sauce*

---

> **FREEZING POULTRY**
> ✧ Frozen poultry should not have a layer of ice around the bird. This indicates that the bird has been thawed and refrozen.
> ✧ Completely thaw frozen birds before cooking and make sure that all the ice crystals are removed.
> ✧ To thaw birds place them in the bottom of the refrigerator for 24-36 hours, or thaw in the microwave oven on DEFROST (30%) for 10-15 minutes per 1 pound (500 g) of chicken.

## CHEESY CHICKEN ROLLS

Serves 6

- ☐ **2 tablespoons olive oil**
- ☐ **2 cloves garlic, crushed**
- ☐ **4 boned, skinned chicken breast halves, cut into thin strips**
- ☐ **4 oz (125 g) button mushrooms, sliced**
- ☐ **1 cup (60 g) fresh bread crumbs**
- ☐ **1 cup (250 g) ricotta cheese**
- ☐ **1 tablespoon chopped fresh parsley**
- ☐ **1 tablespoon chopped fresh chives**
- ☐ **freshly ground black pepper**
- ☐ **3 sheets ready-rolled puff pastry**
- ☐ **1 egg, lightly beaten**

1   Heat oil in a nonstick skillet and cook garlic and chicken in three separate batches over medium heat for 3-5 minutes, or until chicken is cooked. Remove from pan, drain and set aside.
2   Add mushrooms to pan and cook for 3-4 minutes. Combine chicken, mushrooms, bread crumbs, cheese, parsley and chives. Season to taste with pepper.
3   Cut pastry sheets in half crosswise and divide mixture between them. Brush edges of pastry with water and fold up to form a parcel. Place onto a wetted cookie sheet, brush with egg and bake at 350°F (180°C) for 30 minutes or until golden brown.

---

## CHICKEN WITH ALMONDS AND HERBS

*A variation on the world famous Russian Chicken Kiev, this recipe adds mustard and chopped almonds to give an interesting combination of flavors.*

Serves 4

- ☐ **4 boned, skinned chicken breast halves**
- ☐ **oil for cooking**

COATING
- ☐ **¹/₂ cup (60 g) all-purpose flour seasoned with freshly ground black pepper**
- ☐ **2 eggs, lightly beaten with 4 tablespoons milk**
- ☐ **2 cups (125 g) soft white bread crumbs**

HERB BUTTER
- ☐ **³/₄ cup (1¹/₂ sticks/185 g) butter, softened**
- ☐ **3 tablespoons (60 g) almonds, chopped**
- ☐ **2 teaspoons French mustard**
- ☐ **1 tablespoon chopped fresh parsley**
- ☐ **1 tablespoon chopped fresh chives**
- ☐ **freshly ground black pepper**

1   To make herb butter, combine butter, almonds, mustard, parsley and chives. Season to taste with pepper. Divide mixture into four portions and shape into rolls 4 inches (10 cm) long. Refrigerate until firm.
2   Remove all visible fat from chicken. Place halves between two pieces of plastic food wrap and pound with a rolling pin to flatten. Take care not to put a hole in the flesh or the butter will run out during cooking.
3   Place a butter roll in the center of each breast half. Fold the shorter ends into the center and then roll up to fully encase the butter. Secure edges with wooden picks.
4   To coat, roll chicken in flour, dip in egg mixture and roll in bread crumbs. Repeat egg and bread crumb steps. Cover and refrigerate for 1 hour.
5   Heat oil in a large saucepan and cook chicken for 5-8 minutes or until golden brown and cooked through.

> **COOK'S TIP**
> Do not allow the oil to become too hot when cooking crumbed foods or the coating will brown before the chicken is cooked.

**COOK'S TIP**
The flesh of fresh whole birds should be a white-pink color, plump and smooth looking, and the bird should have pliable leg and breast bones.

# Seafood

In these health-conscious times, fish is becoming increasingly popular. It is low in fat and high in protein, quick and easy to cook and perfect for microwaving.

## THAI FISH

*These broiled fish with their spicy flavor are sure to become a favorite.*

Serves 4

- [ ] **4 small whole fish**

MARINADE
- [ ] **2 small red chilies, seeded and finely chopped**
- [ ] **1 clove garlic, crushed**
- [ ] **2 teaspoons grated fresh ginger**
- [ ] **1¹/₂ tablespoons chopped fresh coriander**
- [ ] **2 tablespoons lime juice**
- [ ] **2 tablespoons peanut oil**
- [ ] **1 teaspoon ground cumin**
- [ ] **freshly ground black pepper**

1  Rinse fish under cold running water and pat dry with paper towels. Score flesh with a sharp knife to make 2-3 diagonal cuts along the body. Place in a shallow dish.

2  To make marinade, combine chili, garlic, ginger, coriander, lime juice, oil and cumin in a small bowl. Season to taste with pepper. Pour over fish and rub well into the flesh. Cover and marinate for 2 hours, or preferably overnight in the refrigerator.

3  Remove fish from marinade and broil under a medium heat for 8-10 minutes, or until fish flakes when tested with a fork. Baste frequently with marinade and turn halfway through cooking.

---

### COOK'S TIP

✧ These tasty fish are also great barbecued or pan cooked.

✧ Fish is cooked when it flakes easily when tested with a fork; if it is overcooked it will be dry and tough.

---

*Spicy Seafood Cakes, Baked Stuffed Fish, Thai Fish*

## BAKED STUFFED FISH

*Whole white-fleshed fish, such as snapper, is suitable to use in this recipe.*

Serves 4

- [ ] **1 tablespoon olive oil**
- [ ] **1 small onion, finely chopped**
- [ ] **1 clove garlic, crushed**
- [ ] **3 spinach leaves, stalks removed and leaves finely shredded**
- [ ] **3 strips bacon, finely chopped**
- [ ] **2 tablespoons currants**
- [ ] **2 tablespoons pine nuts, toasted**
- [ ] **1 cup (60 g) soft bread crumbs**
- [ ] **1 egg, lightly beaten**
- [ ] **2 teaspoons lemon juice**
- [ ] **1 tablespoon chopped fresh parsley**
- [ ] **1 tablespoon chopped fresh rosemary**
- [ ] **freshly ground black pepper**
- [ ] **2 whole fish, about 1¹/₄ pounds (600 g) each, cleaned and scaled**
- [ ] **1 cup (250 mL) dry white wine**
- [ ] **¹/₄ cup (¹/₂ stick/60 g) butter, melted**

1  Heat oil in a nonstick skillet and cook onion and garlic for 3-4 minutes or until onion softens. Add spinach and bacon and cook for 5 minutes longer, or until spinach wilts. Remove from heat.

2  Combine spinach mixture, currants, pine nuts, bread crumbs, egg, lemon juice, parsley and rosemary in a large bowl. Season to taste with pepper and mix well.

3  Divide mixture into two portions and fill the cavities of each fish. Close securely, using skewers or wooden picks. Place in a greased shallow baking dish, pour wine over and brush fish with butter.

4  Bake at 350°F (180°C) for 35-40 minutes, or until fish flakes when tested with a fork. Baste frequently during cooking.

## SPICY SEAFOOD CAKES

Serves 4

- [ ] **1 pound (500 g) potatoes, peeled and chopped**
- [ ] **1 cup (250 mL) water**
- [ ] **2 lime leaves**
- [ ] **5 oz (150 g) uncooked shrimp, shelled and deveined**
- [ ] **3 oz (100 g) scallops**
- [ ] **8 oz (250 g) white fish fillets**
- [ ] **¹/₂ cup (60 g) shredded Cheddar cheese**
- [ ] **2 tablespoons all-purpose flour**
- [ ] **2 eggs, lightly beaten**
- [ ] **1 tablespoon lemon juice**
- [ ] **2 tablespoons lime juice**
- [ ] **2 teaspoons grated lemon rind**
- [ ] **1 small red chili, seeded and finely chopped**
- [ ] **1 tablespoon finely chopped fresh coriander**
- [ ] **freshly ground black pepper to taste**
- [ ] **1 cup (125 g) dry bread crumbs**
- [ ] **¹/₂ cup (125 mL) polyunsaturated oil**

PLUM SAUCE
- [ ] **4 tablespoons fruit chutney, large pieces chopped**
- [ ] **¹/₂ cup (130 g) plum jam**
- [ ] **1 tablespoon red wine vinegar**
- [ ] **1 teaspoon Chinese five spice**

1  Boil, steam or microwave potatoes until tender. Drain well and mash.

2  Place water and lime leaves in a skillet and heat over a medium heat until simmering. Reduce heat, add shrimp and scallops and cook for 2-3 minutes or until shrimp just change color. Remove seafood from liquid and drain on paper towels. Place in a food processor or blender and process until smooth.

3  Bring liquid back to the simmer and cook fish for 10-15 minutes, or until it flakes when tested with a fork. Remove pan from heat and allow fish to cool in the liquid. When cool, remove from pan and flake with a fork.

4  Combine potato, shrimp mixture, fish, cheese, flour, eggs, lemon and lime juices, lemon rind, chili and coriander in a large bowl and mix well. Season to taste with pepper. Shape mixture into eight patties, coat with bread crumbs and refrigerate for 30 minutes.

5  Heat oil in a skillet and cook patties until golden brown on each side. Drain on paper towels.

6  To make sauce, place chutney, jam, vinegar and five spice in saucepan. Bring to the boil, stirring constantly, and simmer for 5 minutes. Serve with seafood cakes.

## FISH BURGERS

*A boneless fillet of fish in a burger is the perfect way to introduce your family to the delicate flavor and texture of fish.*

Serves 4

- ☐ **2 teaspoons vegetable oil**
- ☐ **4 x 3 oz (90 g) white fish fillets**
- ☐ **4 wholewheat hamburger buns, cut in half**
- ☐ **4 lettuce leaves, shredded**
- ☐ **2 tomatoes, sliced**
- ☐ **1 small cucumber, sliced**
- ☐ **1 tablespoon mayonnaise**
- ☐ **2 tablespoons plain yogurt**
- ☐ **1 tablespoon finely chopped fresh chives**
- ☐ **freshly ground black pepper**

1  Heat oil in a nonstick skillet and cook fish fillets for 2-3 minutes each side or until flesh flakes easily when tested with a fork. Set aside and keep warm.

2  Toast hamburger buns and top bottom half with lettuce, tomatoes and cucumber.

3  Combine mayonnaise, yogurt and chives and place a spoonful on each burger. Top with fish, season to taste with pepper and cover with top of bun.

## GOLDEN OAT FISH FILLETS

*This recipe can be made with any white-fleshed fish. Lemon pepper seasoning is a mixture of black pepper, salt, sugar, lemon peel and lemon extract.*

Serves 4

- ☐ **3 tablespoons fine oatmeal**
- ☐ **$^2/_3$ cup (60 g) rolled oats**
- ☐ **1 cup (60 g) soft bread crumbs**
- ☐ **$^1/_2$ teaspoon lemon pepper**
- ☐ **all-purpose flour**
- ☐ **1 egg, beaten**
- ☐ **4 firm white fish fillets**
- ☐ **2 tablespoons (30 g) butter**
- ☐ **1 tablespoon vegetable oil**
- ☐ **lemon wedges**

1  Combine oatmeal, oats, bread crumbs and lemon pepper. Coat fish with flour, dip in beaten egg and coat well with crumb mixture.

2  Heat butter and oil in a skillet over a medium heat, cook fish for 3-4 minutes each side or until golden and cooked through. Serve with lemon wedges.

## LEMON FISH PARCELS

Serves 4

- ☐ **4 large white fish fillets**
- ☐ **1 tablespoon finely chopped capers**
- ☐ **$^1/_2$ cup (125 mL) lemon juice**
- ☐ **freshly ground black pepper**
- ☐ **8 fresh, cooked or canned asparagus spears**
- ☐ **$^1/_2$ teaspoon paprika**

1  Lightly grease four sheets of aluminum foil and place a fish fillet in the centre of each sheet.

2  Top each fillet with a teaspoon of capers. Pour over lemon juice and season with pepper. Place two asparagus spears over each fillet and dust lightly with paprika.

3  Fold up edges of aluminum foil to completely encase fish. Place parcels on a cookie sheet and bake at 350°F (180°C) for 15-20 minutes, or until fish flakes when tested with a fork. Remove fish from foil to serve.

*Golden Oat Fish Fillets*

## FISH STEAKS WITH ITALIAN SAUCE

Serves 4

- [ ] 4 x 5 oz (155 g) white fish steaks
- [ ] 2 tablespoons lemon juice
- [ ] 6 green onions, finely chopped
- [ ] 1 clove garlic, crushed
- [ ] 14 oz (440 g) canned tomatoes, undrained and mashed
- [ ] 7 oz (220 g) button mushrooms, sliced
- [ ] $^1/_2$ cup (125 mL) red wine
- [ ] 2 teaspoons finely chopped fresh basil or $^1/_2$ teaspoon dried basil
- [ ] $^1/_2$ teaspoon dried oregano
- [ ] freshly ground black pepper
- [ ] 2 tablespoons grated Parmesan cheese

1  Brush fish steaks with lemon juice. Cook under a preheated medium grill for 4-5 minutes each side. Set aside and keep warm.

2  Place green onions, garlic, tomatoes, mushrooms, wine, basil, oregano and pepper to taste in a saucepan and bring to a boil. Reduce heat and simmer gently for 8-10 minutes.

3  Arrange fish steaks on serving plates. Spoon sauce over and top with Parmesan cheese.

## MARINATED FISH AND AVOCADO SALAD

*A delicious Mexican way of serving fish. The citrus juice 'cooks' the fish as it marinates, making it firm and white.*

Serves 4

- [ ] 1 pound (500 g) firm white fish fillets, skinned and cut into thin strips
- [ ] 4 tablespoons lime juice
- [ ] 4 tablespoons lemon juice
- [ ] 2 tablespoons chopped fresh parsley
- [ ] lettuce leaves

RED PEPPER SEASONING DRESSING
- [ ] 1 clove garlic, crushed
- [ ] $^1/_2$ cup (125 mL) olive oil
- [ ] freshly ground black pepper
- [ ] 6 drops red pepper seasoning or to taste

TOMATO SALAD
- [ ] 4 tomatoes, cut into eighths
- [ ] 6 green onions, sliced lengthwise
- [ ] 1 green pepper, thinly sliced
- [ ] 2 avocados, pitted, peeled and diced

1  Place fish in a bowl and pour over lime and lemon juices. Toss well, cover and refrigerate for 4-6 hours.

2  To make dressing, place garlic, oil, black pepper to taste and red pepper seasoning in a screwtop jar. Shake well to combine.

3  To make salad, place tomatoes, green onions, green pepper and avocados in a bowl. Pour dressing over salad and toss to combine.

4  To serve, arrange lettuce leaves on four serving plates and top with salad. Drain fish and discard marinade. Arrange fish on salad and sprinkle with parsley.

*Fish Steaks with Italian Sauce*

45

# Take a fish cutlet

A steak is a cross-sectional slice of a fish. In the following recipes the steaks are pan cooked and served with the sauce of your choice.

## BUYING FISH

✧ When buying fish it should have firm flesh and a pleasant sea smell.
✧ Whole fish should also have bright and full eyes, bright red gills and a bright and glossy skin.
✧ Quantities to allow per serving:
Whole fish: 10-12 oz (290-350 g)
Whole fish with head removed and cleaned: 7-9 oz (225-275 g)
Fish fillets: 3-5 oz (100-175 g)
Fish steaks: 5-7 oz (175-225 g)

## FISH STEAKS WITH ONE OF THREE SAUCES

Serves 4

☐ **1 tablespoon olive oil**
☐ **1 tablespoon (30 g) butter**
☐ **4 fish steaks**

Heat oil and butter in a large nonstick skillet. Cook steaks over medium heat for 3-5 minutes, or until fish flakes with a fork, turning once during cooking.

## CREAMY APRICOT SAUCE

☐ **5 oz (150 g) canned apricots, drained and chopped**
☐ **$^1/_4$ cup (40 g) blanched almonds, chopped**
☐ **$^1/_2$ cup (125 g) ricotta cheese**
☐ **1 tablespoon dry sherry**
☐ **$^1/_2$ cup (125 mL) cream**
☐ **2 teaspoons Grand Marnier**
☐ **1 tablespoon lemon juice**
☐ **freshly ground black pepper**

1 Place apricots, almonds, ricotta and sherry in a food processor or blender and process until smooth. Stir in cream and Grand Marnier.
2 Transfer mixture to a small saucepan and heat through. Stir in lemon juice and season to taste with pepper.

## TARTAR SAUCE

☐ **1 cup (250 mL) mayonnaise**
☐ **2 tablespoons finely chopped sweet pickles**
☐ **1 tablespoon chopped capers**
☐ **2 teaspoons finely chopped fresh parsley**
☐ **1 teaspoon chopped fresh dill**

Combine mayonnaise, pickles, capers, parsley and dill in a bowl and mix well.

## ❖ SPICY SEAFOOD SAUCE

- ☐ **2 tablespoons (30 g) butter**
- ☐ **2 tablespoons all-purpose flour**
- ☐ **1 cup (250 mL) chicken stock or broth**
- ☐ **1 cup (250 mL) milk**
- ☐ **1 teaspoon Worcestershire sauce**
- ☐ **3 drops red pepper seasoning**
- ☐ **1 tablespoon cream**
- ☐ **1 1/2 tablespoons tomato paste**
- ☐ **2 oz (50 g) mussels meat, chopped**
- ☐ **3 oz (100 g) shrimp, shelled and deveined**
- ☐ **2 teaspoons chopped fresh parsley**
- ☐ **2 tablespoons lemon juice**
- ☐ **1 tablespoon mayonnaise**
- ☐ **freshly ground black pepper**

1   Melt butter in a saucepan. Stir in flour and cook for 1 minute. Remove from heat and gradually whisk in stock or broth and milk. Return to heat, stirring constantly until mixture boils and thickens.

2   Add Worcestershire sauce, red pepper seasoning, cream, tomato paste, mussels, shrimp, parsley, lemon juice and mayonnaise and heat through. Season to taste with pepper.

*Fish Steaks with Creamy Apricot Sauce, Spicy Seafood Sauce, Tartar Sauce*

## MICROWAVE IT

✧ Fish and the microwave oven are perfect partners. The easiest way to cook fish in the microwave oven is to place the required number of fish fillets in a shallow microwave-safe dish, sprinkle with lemon juice and chopped fresh herbs of your choice and season with freshly ground black pepper. Cover with microwave-safe plastic food wrap and cook on HIGH (100%) for 4-5 minutes per pound (500 g) of fish.

✧ Whole fish cook well in the microwave oven – their eyes should be removed before cooking as they will explode. Whole fish is best cooked on a MEDIUM-HIGH (70%) power setting, allowing 5-6 minutes per pound (500 g) of fish.

✧ When cooking shellfish in the microwave oven, use a MEDIUM-HIGH (70%) power setting, or cook them in a liquid or sauce. Shellfish have a high moisture content and tend to "pop" during cooking and will easily overcook if care is not taken. One of the easiest ways to cook shellfish is to make your sauce or heat the liquid then drop the fish in. Only a very short cooking time is then required.

## Storing fish

**Whole fish, steaks and fillets:** Wash under cold running water and dry well with paper towels. Place in covered container or wrap in foil and store in refrigerator. Whole fish will keep for 2-3 days. Steaks and fillets will keep approximately 1-2 days.

**Shellfish:** Place in a covered container and refrigerate and use within 1-2 days. Before storing mussels and clams, prepare by removing beard and scrubbing shells under cold running water. If storing live mollusks, such as mussels, clams, oysters or cockles, do not refrigerate, as this causes them to die. They are best stored in a slightly damp cloth bag in a cool, dark place. They can be stored in this way for up to 3 days in cool weather. Before cooking, discard any that have opened.

## Freezing fish

✧ Freeze only the freshest fish.

✧ Freeze whole fish only if you intend to cook it whole; thawed fish is difficult to fillet. Ensure that all portions to be frozen are clean. Wrap in plastic food wrap, or seal in a freezer bag. Name and date, then freeze.

✧ Dip the fish in cold water as soon as it is frozen and return to the freezer. This will form an ice seal which helps prevent the fish from becoming dry and "off" flavors developing.

✧ White fish can be frozen for 4-6 months.

✧ Oily fish, such as salmon, trout and mackerel, should not be frozen for longer than 2 months.

✧ Fish is best cooked in its frozen state. On thawing it loses a large proportion of its natural juices and flavor. As fish only takes a short time to cook you do not have to worry about the problems associated with cooking frozen meats and poultry.

*Spoons from The Bay Tree*

## COURT BOUILLON

*This liquid is used for poaching fish.*

- ☐ **4 cups (1 litre) water**
- ☐ **1 stalk celery, chopped**
- ☐ **1 carrot, chopped**
- ☐ **4 tablespoons white wine vinegar**
- ☐ **1 bay leaf**
- ☐ **6 peppercorns**
- ☐ **sprig fresh thyme**

Place water, celery, carrot, vinegar, bay leaf, peppercorns and thyme in a medium saucepan. Bring to the boil and simmer for 15-20 minutes. Strain liquid and use as desired.

# Take a potato

The humble potato is a meal in itself when baked and filled with a tasty stuffing, or it is a nutritious vegetable accompaniment roasted, boiled, mashed, or fried.

## THE PERFECT FRY

*Double-cooking french fries ensures crisp golden results every time. The high water content of potatoes initially reduces the temperature of the oil and double-cooking overcomes this problem. A wire fry basket makes it easier to lower and raise a quantity of potatoes in hot oil. If cooking a large quantity, cook in batches to prevent overcrowding.*

Serves 4

- ☐ **4 large potatoes, peeled and washed**
- ☐ **oil for cooking**

1  Cut potatoes into $1/2$-inch (1 cm) slices, then into strips. Soak strips in cold water for 10 minutes to remove the excess starch. Drain and dry on paper towels.
2  Heat oil in a deep saucepan. Drop a potato strip into the oil and when it rises to the surface surrounded by bubbles the oil is at the correct temperature for cooking. Drop the potatoes gradually into the hot oil, or lower them in a wire basket and cook for 6 minutes.
3  Remove potatoes from oil using a slotted spoon, or by lifting the basket, and drain on paper towels. At this point the potatoes are blanched and can be left for several hours, or frozen before the final cooking stage.
4  Just prior to serving, reheat the oil and test as above. Cook fries quickly for 3-4 minutes or until golden brown and crisp. Remove from pan with a slotted spoon, drain on paper towels. Season to taste and serve immediately.

❖

## BAKED JACKET POTATOES

*Baked potatoes can be placed in the oven and cooked with other dishes. If the other food you are cooking requires a slightly lower or higher temperature your baked potatoes will happily cook along with it taking just a little shorter or longer time as the case may be.*

Serves 4

- ☐ **4 potatoes**
- ☐ **sour cream or butter for serving**

Scrub and dry potatoes. Pierce with a fork and place directly on oven shelf, or on a roasting rack in a baking dish. Bake at 350°F (180°C) for 1 hour or until tender. Serve with sour cream or butter.

❖

## BACON AND CREAMED CORN FILLED POTATOES

*You will require only half the potato flesh for this recipe. Reserve the remaining flesh for another use. Leftover potato can be made into potato cakes or croquettes, or can be pan cooked.*

Serves 4

- ☐ **4 potatoes, baked in their jackets**
- ☐ **4 strips bacon, chopped**
- ☐ **4 oz (130 g) canned creamed corn**
- ☐ **2 tablespoons sour cream**
- ☐ **pinch chili powder**
- ☐ **$1/2$ cup (60 g) shredded Cheddar cheese**

1  Cut potatoes in half, scoop out flesh, leaving a $1/2$-inch (1 cm) thick shell. Reserve the flesh and set aside.
2  Cook the bacon in a nonstick skillet for 2-3 minutes or until crisp. Mash half the potato flesh and combine with bacon, corn, sour cream and chili powder. Spoon mixture into potato shells. Top with cheese.
3  Place potatoes on a cookie sheet and bake at 350°F (180°C) for 15 minutes or until cheese melts.

## PERFECT ROAST POTATOES

*When roasting vegetables use a shallow baking dish, which will allow the vegetables to brown evenly. Other vegetables can be roasted with the potatoes. Cook butternut squash with or without the skin and cut into a similar size as the potatoes. Yellow onions are excellent roasted; peel away 1 or 2 layers of skin, leaving a little of the root end intact to hold onions together during cooking.*

- ☐ **4 potatoes, peeled and halved**
- ☐ **1 tablespoon polyunsaturated oil**

1  Boil or steam potatoes for 5 minutes. Drain and dry on paper towels. Set aside until cool enough to handle, then cut in half lengthwise. Score the upper rounded surface with a fork; this helps crisp the potatoes during cooking.
2  Brush potatoes with oil and place in a shallow baking dish and bake at 350°F (180°C) for 55-60 minutes, turning occasionally during cooking.

❖

## POTATO AND BEET TART

*This vibrantly-colored dish will give any meal a lift. It may be served either hot or cold.*

Serves 4

- ☐ **4 potatoes, cooked and mashed (without milk or butter)**
- ☐ **1 large raw beet, shredded**
- ☐ **1 tablespoon finely chopped fresh dill**
- ☐ **1 tablespoon cream**
- ☐ **1 tablespoon mayonnaise**
- ☐ **2 teaspoons bottled horseradish**
- ☐ **freshly ground black pepper**
- ☐ **2 eggs, separated**

1  Combine potatoes, beet, dill, cream, mayonnaise, horseradish, pepper and egg yolks in a mixing bowl.
2  Beat egg whites until stiff peaks form and fold through potato mixture. Spoon mixture into a well-greased 9-inch (23 cm) tart pan with a removable base. Bake at 400°F (200°C) for 25-30 minutes or until firm. Serve warm, or at room temperature, cut into wedges.

## BACON AND BANANA POTATO CAKES

Serves 4

- ☐ **4 potatoes, cooked and mashed (without milk or butter)**
- ☐ **1 small green apple, shredded**
- ☐ **1 tablespoon mayonnaise**
- ☐ **2 teaspoons chopped fresh mint**
- ☐ **3 tablespoons all-purpose flour**

FILLING
- ☐ **4 strips bacon, finely chopped**
- ☐ **1 banana, sliced**

COATING
- ☐ **all-purpose flour**
- ☐ **1 egg, lightly beaten**
- ☐ **1 cup (125 g) dry bread crumbs**
- ☐ **oil for cooking**

1   Combine potato, apple, mayonnaise, mint and flour. Divide potato mixture into sixteen equal portions and form into patties.

2   To make filling, cook bacon in a nonstick skillet for 2-3 minutes or until crisp. Set aside to cool slightly. Place a spoonful of bacon on eight of the patties. Top with banana slices and remaining potato patties. Mold potato patties to completely seal filling.

3   To coat, cover patties lightly with flour, dip in egg, then bread crumbs. Refrigerate for 30 minutes.

4   Heat oil in a skillet and cook patties, two at a time, until golden brown on both sides. Remove from pan and drain on paper towels. Set aside and keep warm. Cook remaining patties.

---

## PERFECT MASHED POTATO

Serves 4

- ☐ **4 potatoes, peeled and halved**
- ☐ **1/2 cup (125 mL) milk**
- ☐ **2 tablespoons (30 g) butter, softened**

1   Place potatoes in a saucepan of water, cover and bring to the boil. Cook gently for 20 minutes or until tender.

2   Drain potatoes, then return to pan. Shake pan over low heat to dry. Mash potatoes until free of lumps.

3   Stir in milk and butter. Season to taste and beat with a fork until smooth and fluffy.

---

*Top: Potato and Beet Tart*
*Centre: Baked Jacket Potatoes, Bacon and Creamed Corn Filled Potatoes*
*Bottom: Bacon and Banana Potato Cakes*

# Saucy vegetables

Fresh vegetables, cooked or raw, are the tastiest and healthiest foods you can eat. Try new recipes or your favorite vegetables topped with a delicious sauce.

❖

## BASIC WHITE SAUCE

*Sauces are the perfect accompaniment for vegetables. The following Basic White Sauce recipe and its variations can be served with many different steamed, boiled or microwaved vegetables.*

Makes 1 cup (250 mL)

- ☐ **2 tablespoons (30 g) butter**
- ☐ **2 tablespoons all-purpose flour**
- ☐ **¼ teaspoon dry mustard**
- ☐ **1 cup (250 mL) milk**

1   Melt butter in a saucepan, then stir in flour and mustard. Cook over medium heat for 1 minute.

2   Remove pan from heat and whisk in milk a little at a time until well blended. Cook over medium heat, stirring constantly until sauce boils and thickens.

### Variations

**Cheese Sauce:** When the sauce thickens, stir in ½ cup (60 g) shredded Cheddar cheese. Serve immediately. Avoid reheating after the cheese is added or it becomes tough and stringy.

---

### CAULIFLOWER AU GRATIN
Use the Cheese Sauce and make a vegetable au gratin. For example, place steamed cauliflower in a shallow ovenproof dish, pour Cheese Sauce over. Top with shredded cheese and bake at 350°F (180°C) for 15-20 minutes.

---

**Mushroom Sauce:** Melt the butter and cook 3 oz (100 g) sliced button mushrooms for 4-5 minutes. Remove mushrooms from pan and set aside. Continue making as for Basic White Sauce, replacing 3 tablespoons of milk with cream. When sauce thickens, return mushrooms to the pan and heat through.

**Mustard Sauce:** Blend 2 teaspoons of dry mustard and 1 tablespoon sugar into the flour mixture. When sauce thickens stir in 1 tablespoon white vinegar.

**Herb Sauce:** When sauce thickens remove from heat and stir in 2 tablespoons finely chopped fresh parsley, 1 tablespoon finely chopped chives and 1 tablespoon finely chopped dill.

**Curry Sauce:** Blend 2 teaspoons of curry powder into the flour mixture and cook as for Basic White Sauce.

---

## THE PERFECT DRESSING

### VINAIGRETTE

Makes 1 cup (250 mL)

- ☐ **1 tablespoon French mustard**
- ☐ **3 tablespoons white wine vinegar**
- ☐ **freshly ground black pepper**
- ☐ **¾ cup (190 mL) olive oil**

Place mustard in a bowl and whisk in the vinegar. Season to taste with pepper. Add the oil a little at a time, whisking well until mixture thickens.

### MAYONNAISE

Makes 2 cups (500 mL)

- ☐ **3 egg yolks**
- ☐ **1 tablespoon Dijon-style mustard**
- ☐ **freshly ground black pepper**
- ☐ **2 tablespoons lemon juice**
- ☐ **2 cups (500 mL) olive oil**

Place egg yolks, mustard, pepper to taste and lemon juice in a food processor or blender and process for 1 minute. With the machine running, add the oil in a slow, steady stream. When all of the oil is incorporated, scrape down the sides of the bowl. Transfer mixture to a glass bowl, cover and refrigerate until required.

## Vegetable preparation

✧ Vegetables need little preparation and where possible you should scrub rather than peel them. Many important vitamins are contained just under the skin.

✧ As many of the nutrients in vegetables are water soluble they are lost if the vegetables are soaked for a long time.

✧ Wash vegetables under cold running water just long enough to remove any dirt. Prepare and cook them immediately.

✧ Once cut and exposed to the air the goodness rapidly disappears.

✧ Cook vegetables in a minimal amount of water for a short time; this will keep vitamin loss to a minimum.

✧ Steaming or microwaving retains the most nutrients, as the cooking time is short and a minimal quantity of water is used.

✧ If boiling vegetables, the rule is to cook root vegetables in cold water with the lid on, and plunge green vegetables into hot water and cook with the lid off; then refresh under cold water to retain the color and stop the cooking.

✧ An easy and tasty idea for serving hot vegetables, is to toss them in a vinaigrette dressing. Try using different vinegars, or lemon juice. Herb and fruit vinegars are popular alternatives.

## Buying and storing vegetables

✧ Vegetables are at their best when first picked.

✧ When you are buying vegetables, choose produce without blemishes, bruises or marks.

✧ Most vegetables are best stored in the vegetable section of the refrigerator.

✧ Store tuber-type vegetables, such as potatoes, in a dry dark place like a pantry cupboard.

✧ The storage time of vegetables will greatly depend on their condition when purchased.

✧ Cover cut vegetables with plastic food wrap to prevent vitamin loss, keep the surface moist and prevent aromas in the refrigerator.

✧ Carrots and parsnips will keep for several weeks if you wrap them in paper towels, place them in a plastic freezer bag and keep in the vegetable section of the refrigerator.

## NUTRITIOUS VEGETABLES

✧ Some of the important nutrients contained in vegetables are vitamin A, vitamin B, vitamin C, potassium, iron and magnesium. Vegetables also provide dietary fiber and complex carbohydrates.

✧ When compared by weight the vegetable which is lowest in calories (kilojoules) is celery, followed closely by cucumber and lettuce. Three long stalks of celery, 20 lettuce leaves, or half a cucumber, contain the same calories as half a slice of bread.

# Take a leaf

What goes into a salad to make it green? Nowadays there are many tasty greens available to make your salads something special.

## ❖ ENDIVE, ROMAINE, TUNA AND OLIVE SALAD

Serves 4

- ☐ 1 bunch curly endive, leaves separated and washed
- ☐ 1 romaine lettuce, leaves separated and washed
- ☐ 1 cup (125 g) cherry tomatoes, halved
- ☐ 5 oz (150 g) green beans, trimmed and blanched
- ☐ 8 small new potatoes, cooked and halved
- ☐ 3 hard-boiled eggs, quartered
- ☐ 4 green onions, chopped
- ☐ $^1/_2$ red pepper, cut into thin strips
- ☐ $^1/_2$ green pepper, cut into thin strips
- ☐ 12 pitted black olives
- ☐ 14 oz (440 g) canned tuna, drained and flaked
- ☐ 3 tablespoons finely chopped parsley

DRESSING
- ☐ 1 clove garlic, crushed
- ☐ 4 anchovy fillets, drained
- ☐ freshly ground black pepper
- ☐ $^1/_4$ teaspoon sugar
- ☐ 2 teaspoons finely chopped fresh basil
- ☐ 2 tablespoons cider vinegar
- ☐ 4 tablespoons olive oil

1   Arrange endive and romaine lettuce in a large salad bowl. Combine tomatoes, beans, potatoes, eggs, green onions, red and green pepper, olives, tuna and parsley, and arrange attractively over lettuce.

2   To make dressing, place garlic, anchovies, peppers, sugar, basil, vinegar and oil in a food processor or blender and process until all ingredients are combined. Pour over salad and serve.

## ❖ BLUE CHEESE AND WALDORF SALAD

Serves 6

- ☐ 3 oz (90 g) blue cheese, crumbled
- ☐ $^3/_4$ cup (120 g) pecan nuts, chopped
- ☐ 1 red apple, cored and thinly sliced
- ☐ 1 green apple, cored and thinly sliced
- ☐ 1 stalk celery, sliced
- ☐ 1 head radicchio, leaves separated and washed
- ☐ bunch watercress

DRESSING
- ☐ 2 teaspoons Dijon-style mustard
- ☐ 2 tablespoons red wine vinegar
- ☐ 1 tablespoon port wine
- ☐ $^1/_2$ cup (125 mL) grapeseed oil

1   Combine cheese, pecans, red and green apples and celery in a bowl. Line a salad bowl with radicchio leaves and watercress and refrigerate.

2   To make dressing, combine mustard, vinegar, port and oil in a screwtop jar. Shake to combine all ingredients. Pour half the dressing over apple mixture and toss. Spoon apple salad over leaves, then pour remaining dressing over and serve.

*Endive, Romaine, Tuna and Olive Salad, Blue Cheese and Waldorf Salad, Three Grains with Spinach and Chicken, Beet and Fennel Parcels*

## KNOWING YOUR GREENS

**Chicory or Witloof (Belgian Endive):**
Tightly clustered, smooth white leaves with yellow tips. Slightly bitter flavor.

**Curly Endive:** Sold in large bunches. The long leaves graduate from pale, greeny yellow to dark green. Use only the paler heart and stalks. Bitter flavor.

**Bibb or Boston lettuce:** Soft, smallish lettuce. Mild flavor.

**Romaine lettuce:** Elongated head of dark green oval leaves and a crisp pale green heart. Has a pungent flavor and stays crisp.

**Iceberg or Crisp Head lettuce:** A large lettuce with crisp outer leaves and a firm, sweet heart. The basis of many salads as the leaves stay crisp.

**Mignonette lettuce:** Soft, smallish leaves with edges tinged pink to red.

**Radicchio:** Beet-colored with white veins and tightly packed heads.

**Rocket:** Small, acidic, dark green leaves. It is sold while the plant is still very young.

**English spinach:** Dark green leaves. Eaten raw in salads when leaves are young and fresh.

**Watercress:** Use only young outer leaves and tender stems for salads. The remainder can be used in soups. Pungent, slightly peppery flavor.

## BEET AND FENNEL PARCELS

Serves 4

- ☐ 8 large lettuce leaves
- ☐ 1 large raw beet, peeled and cut into thin strips
- ☐ 1 fennel bulb, cut into thin strips
- ☐ 1 red onion, sliced

DRESSING
- ☐ 1 cup (200 g) light sour cream
- ☐ 4 anchovy fillets, drained
- ☐ 2 tablespoons white wine vinegar
- ☐ 1 tablespoon finely chopped fresh basil
- ☐ 2 teaspoons olive oil
- ☐ 1/2 teaspoon sugar

1 Bring a large saucepan of water to the boil. Plunge lettuce leaves into boiling water. Remove pan from heat, drain and refresh lettuce under cold running water. Set aside.

2 Boil or steam beet and fennel, separately, for 3 minutes. Drain and refresh under cold running water. Combine beet and fennel with onion and divide into eight equal portions. Place one portion on each lettuce leaf and roll up firmly.

3 To make dressing, place sour cream, anchovy fillets, vinegar, basil, oil and sugar in a food processor or blender and process until smooth. Arrange parcels on a serving plate, pour over dressing and serve.

## THREE GRAINS WITH SPINACH AND CHICKEN

Serves 4

- ☐ 4 cups (1 litre) chicken stock or broth
- ☐ 1/4 cup (50 g) wild rice
- ☐ 1/4 cup (50 g) brown rice
- ☐ 1/4 cup (50 g) white rice
- ☐ 1 large spinach leaf, shredded
- ☐ 4 oz (125 g) button mushrooms, sliced
- ☐ 4 green onions, chopped
- ☐ 1 red pepper, cut into strips
- ☐ 2 tablespoons toasted pine nuts
- ☐ 4 boned, skinned chicken breast halves, cooked and sliced

DRESSING
- ☐ 1/2 cup (125 mL) canned coconut cream
- ☐ 1 teaspoon grated fresh ginger
- ☐ 2 tablespoons white wine vinegar
- ☐ 2 teaspoons brown sugar
- ☐ 1/2 teaspoon curry powder
- ☐ 1/4 teaspoon turmeric

1 Place stock or broth in a large saucepan and bring to the boil. Add wild rice and brown rice and cook for 35-40 minutes or until tender. Add white rice during the last 15 minutes of cooking. Drain and rinse.

2 Place rice in a bowl and toss with spinach, mushrooms, green onions, pepper, pine nuts and chicken.

3 To make dressing, place coconut cream, ginger, vinegar, sugar, curry powder and turmeric in a screwtop jar. Shake well and pour over salad.

# Slaws

The cabbage family includes white cabbage, red, yellow and green savoy and Chinese cabbage. Great for the diet-conscious, cabbage is high in fiber, low in calories (kilojoules), and an excellent source of vitamin C.

Food processor in action

❖
## HOT COLESLAW WITH BRANDY DRESSING

Serves 4

- ☐ **2 strips bacon, chopped**
- ☐ **4-6 cups shredded cabbage**
- ☐ **2 green apples, coarsely chopped**
- ☐ **$1/2$ teaspoon nutmeg**

BRANDY DRESSING
- ☐ **1 clove garlic, crushed**
- ☐ **1 tablespoon cider vinegar**
- ☐ **2 tablespoons brandy**
- ☐ **4 tablespoons walnut oil**
- ☐ **freshly ground black pepper**

1   Cook bacon in a heavy-based skillet until just crisp. Add cabbage and apples and toss well. Cook for 3-4 minutes, then mix in nutmeg. Using a slotted spoon transfer to a warmed bowl and toss to combine.
2   To make dressing, combine garlic, vinegar, brandy, oil and pepper in a screwtop jar and shake well. Pour over coleslaw and serve.

## PINEAPPLE AND KIWIFRUIT SLAW

Serves 6

- ☐ **2-3 cups shredded red cabbage**
- ☐ **3 cups shredded Chinese cabbage**
- ☐ **14 oz (440 g) canned pineapple pieces, drained and juice reserved**
- ☐ **2 kiwifruit, peeled and sliced**
- ☐ **1 red pepper, sliced**
- ☐ **1 green pepper, sliced**

DRESSING
- ☐ **3 tablespoons grapeseed oil**
- ☐ **2 tablespoons reserved pineapple juice**
- ☐ **3 tablespoons finely chopped fresh coriander**
- ☐ **3 tablespoons finely chopped fresh mint**

1   Combine red and Chinese cabbages, pineapple, kiwifruit and red and green peppers in a salad bowl. Toss lightly, cover and refrigerate until required.

2   To make dressing, combine oil, juice, coriander and mint in a screwtop jar. Shake well to combine all ingredients, pour over slaw and serve.

## VEGETABLE SLAW WITH PESTO DRESSING

Serves 6

- ☐ **4-6 cups shredded savoy cabbage**
- ☐ **1 large carrot, cut into thin strips**
- ☐ **4 green onions, chopped**
- ☐ **1 stalk celery, cut into thin strips**
- ☐ **8 radishes, sliced**
- ☐ **1 green pepper, cut into strips**
- ☐ **5 oz (150 g) broccoli florets, cooked**

DRESSING
- ☐ **1 cup (100 g) fresh basil leaves**
- ☐ **2 cloves garlic, crushed**
- ☐ **2 tablespoons pine nuts, toasted**
- ☐ **2 tablespoons grated Parmesan cheese**
- ☐ **5 tablespoons mayonnaise**
- ☐ **3 tablespoons plain yogurt**

1   Place cabbage, carrot, green onions, celery, radishes, pepper and broccoli in a salad bowl. Toss lightly, cover and refrigerate until required.

2   To make dressing, place basil, garlic, pine nuts, Parmesan, mayonnaise and yogurt in a food processor or blender and process until smooth. Pour dressing over slaw and toss lightly.

Bowls and Servers from Bibelot, Laminate from Albet Laminati

## THREE-CABBAGE HOT SLAW

Serves 6

- ☐ **1 tablespoon vegetable oil**
- ☐ **1 tablespoon sesame oil**
- ☐ **1 clove garlic, crushed**
- ☐ **1 teaspoon grated fresh ginger**
- ☐ **1 red chili, seeded and chopped**
- ☐ **1 tablespoon sesame seeds**
- ☐ **2-3 cups shredded red cabbage**
- ☐ **1¹/₂ cups shredded Chinese cabbage**
- ☐ **2-3 cups shredded savoy cabbage**

1   Heat vegetable and sesame oils in a large skillet until very hot. Add garlic, ginger, chili and sesame seeds. Stir-fry for 1 minute.

2   Toss in cabbages and stir-fry for 3-4 minutes or until just cooked.

*Pineapple and Kiwifruit Slaw, Vegetable Slaw with Pesto Dressing, Three-Cabbage Hot Slaw, Hot Coleslaw with Brandy Dressing*

# Sandwich fillers and toppers

Any of the following make great fillers or toppings for snacks or light meals. Serve in or on your favorite bread, roll, bagel, English muffin or croissant.

## SPINACH SLAW

Serves 4

- [ ] **8 oz (250 g) finely shredded spinach leaves**
- [ ] **1 carrot, shredded**
- [ ] **³/4 cup (125 g) golden raisins**
- [ ] **³/4 cup (100 g) roasted peanuts, chopped**
- [ ] **¹/2 cup (125 mL) mayonnaise**
- [ ] **freshly ground black pepper**

Combine spinach, carrot, golden raisins, peanuts and mayonnaise. Season to taste with pepper and use as desired.

## CARAWAY SLAW TOPPING

Serves 4

- [ ] **1¹/2 cups (125 g) finely shredded cabbage**
- [ ] **2 teaspoons caraway seeds**
- [ ] **2 teaspoons coarse grain mustard**
- [ ] **1 tablespoon mayonnaise**
- [ ] **8 slices Swiss cheese**
- [ ] **4 dill pickles, sliced lengthwise**

Combine cabbage, caraway seeds, mustard and mayonnaise. Divide between four slices of bread, then top each slice with 2 slices of cheese and 2 slices of dill pickles.

## CHEESE ASPARAGUS TOPPING

Serves 4

- [ ] **10 oz (315 g) canned asparagus tips, drained**
- [ ] **1 teaspoon coarse grain mustard**
- [ ] **1 tablespoon mayonnaise**
- [ ] **2 oz (60 g) blue cheese, crumbled**

Place asparagus, mustard and mayonnaise in a small bowl and mash to combine. Spread over four slices of bread and sprinkle with cheese.

## BLUE CHEESE AND WALNUTS

Serves 4

- [ ] **6¹/2 oz (200 g) blue cheese, mashed**
- [ ] **1 cup (125 g) walnuts, chopped**
- [ ] **8 romaine lettuce leaves**
- [ ] **1 oz (30 g) alfalfa sprouts**

Combine cheese and walnuts. Line pita pockets, or top bread slices, with lettuce leaves, then top with cheese mixture and alfalfa sprouts.

*From left: Spinach Slaw, Blue Cheese and Walnuts, Rockmelon Camembert Topping, Cheese Asparagus Topping, Caraway Slaw Topping, Tomatoes and Mozzarella, Cool Cucumber Topping, Garden Salad Platter, Mexican Pumpkin Seed Dip*

## GARDEN SALAD PLATTER

*This platter is ideal to serve as a light meal, snack or first course for a barbecue.*

Serves 4

- [ ] 4 slices cheese of your choice
- [ ] 1 large tomato, cut into eighths
- [ ] 1 small cucumber, cut into thin strips
- [ ] 8 canned asparagus spears
- [ ] 8 radishes
- [ ] 2 hard-cooked eggs, sliced
- [ ] 5 oz (155 g) button mushrooms, sliced
- [ ] 1 large stalk celery, cut into thin strips

DILL WEED DIPPING SAUCE
- [ ] 2 tablespoons mayonnaise
- [ ] 1/2 cup (125 mL) plain yogurt
- [ ] 1 teaspoon grated lemon rind
- [ ] 2 tablespoons finely chopped fresh dill weed

1  Arrange cheese slices, tomato, cucumber, asparagus, radishes, eggs, mushrooms and celery attractively on a platter.

2  To make sauce, combine mayonnaise, yogurt, lemon rind and dill weed in a bowl. Mix well to combine and serve with salad platter.

## CANTALOUPE CAMEMBERT TOPPING

Serves 4

- [ ] French mustard
- [ ] aragula leaves
- [ ] 125 g (4 oz) Camembert cheese, sliced
- [ ] 1/2 small cantaloupe, peeled, seeded and diced

Spread each slice of bread with mustard to taste. Top with aragula leaves, Camembert cheese and cantaloupe.

## MEXICAN PUMPKIN SEED DIP

*This dip is delicious served with a vegetable platter.*

Serves 6

- [ ] 1 cup (125 g) pumpkin seeds, toasted
- [ ] 1 tablespoon lemon juice
- [ ] 2 tablespoons balsamic or red wine vinegar
- [ ] 1 clove garlic, crushed
- [ ] 1/2 teaspoon Dijon mustard

Place pumpkin seeds, lemon juice, vinegar, garlic and mustard in a food processor or blender and process until smooth. Chill.

## COOL CUCUMBER TOPPING

Serves 4

- [ ] 1 telegraph cucumber, diced
- [ ] 1/2 cup (125 mL) plain yogurt
- [ ] 1 tablespoon finely chopped fresh dill weed

Combine cucumber, yogurt and dill weed and use as desired.

## TOMATOES AND MOZZARELLA

Serves 4

- [ ] 4 tomatoes, chopped
- [ ] 4 oz (125 g) mozzarella cheese, cubed
- [ ] 2 tablespoons finely chopped fresh basil
- [ ] 3/4 cup (125 g) oz pitted black olives
- [ ] 2 tablespoons cider vinegar
- [ ] 1 tablespoon olive oil
- [ ] freshly ground black pepper

Combine tomatoes, cheese, basil and olives. Mix together vinegar and oil, pour over tomato mixture and toss to combine. Season to taste with pepper and use as desired.

# Take some pasta or rice

Rice and pasta are important staple foods for much of the world's population. Reasonably bland in flavor, they combine well with many other foods.

❖

## SEAFOOD AND TOMATO SAUCE

*Any combination of seafood can be used in this sauce. For a less spicy dish you may wish to omit the chili.*

Serves 4

- [ ] 1 tablespoon olive oil
- [ ] 4 green onions, finely chopped
- [ ] 1 clove garlic, crushed
- [ ] 1 small red chili, finely chopped
- [ ] 1 pound (500 g) cooked shrimp, peeled, deveined and chopped
- [ ] 4 oz (125 g) scallops, halved
- [ ] 14 oz (440 g) canned tomatoes, undrained and mashed
- [ ] 3 tablespoons red wine
- [ ] 3 tablespoons chicken stock or broth
- [ ] 2 teaspoons tomato paste
- [ ] 1 teaspoon sugar
- [ ] 2 teaspoons chopped fresh basil
- [ ] 1 tablespoon chopped fresh parsley
- [ ] 8 oysters in the half-shell

1   Heat oil in a large saucepan and cook green onions, garlic and chili for 1 minute. Stir in shrimp and scallops and cook for 2 minutes longer.

2   Combine tomatoes, wine, stock or broth, tomato paste and sugar and pour into pan with prawn mixture. Bring to the boil, then reduce heat and simmer, uncovered, for 10 minutes.

3   Add basil and parsley. Cook for 2-3 minutes. Spoon sauce over hot, cooked pasta. Garnish with oysters in their shells.

*Coated Chili Rice Balls*

❖

## COATED CHILI RICE BALLS

Makes 16

- [ ] 3  teaspoons olive oil
- [ ] 1 onion, finely chopped
- [ ] 1¼ cups (315 g) long grain rice
- [ ] ½ teaspoon ground turmeric
- [ ] 3 cups (750 mL) chicken stock or broth
- [ ] ½ teaspoon chili powder
- [ ] freshly ground black pepper
- [ ] 3 green onions, finely chopped
- [ ] 1 tablespoon (15 g) butter
- [ ] 3 tablespoons shredded Ch cheese
- [ ] 2 eggs, lightly beaten
- [ ] 4 oz (125 g) mozzarella cheese, cut into ½-inch (1 cm) cubes
- [ ] ¾ cup (90 g) dry bread crumbs
- [ ] oil for cooking

1   Heat oil in a skillet and cook onion for 2-3 minutes or until tender. Stir in rice and turmeric and cook for 1-2 minutes or until rice is coated with oil.

2   Pour in ¾ cup (190 mL) stock or broth and bring to the boil. Cook, stirring frequently until liquid has almost evaporated. Add remaining stock or broth, chili powder and pepper to taste. Simmer for 10-15 minutes or until liquid has been absorbed. Remove pan from heat and stir through green onions, butter and tasty cheese.

3   Lightly fold eggs through, taking care not to mash rice grains. Divide rice mixture into sixteen equal portions. Take a cheese cube and, with hands, mold one portion of rice around cheese to form a ball. Repeat with remaining rice and cheese portions.

4   Coat balls in bread crumbs and refrigerate for 30 minutes. Heat oil in a deep saucepan and cook four to five balls at a time for 5 minutes or until golden. Remove, drain on paper towels and serve.

*Bowls from Lifestyle Imports*

## TUNA AND OLIVE SAUCE

Serves 4

- ☐ **2 tablespoons (30 g) butter**
- ☐ **2 tablespoons all-purpose flour**
- ☐ **¹/₂ cup (125 mL) milk**
- ☐ **3 tablespoons chicken stock or broth**
- ☐ **14 oz (440 g) canned tuna in brine, or water packed tuna, drained and liquid reserved**
- ☐ **1 tablespoon finely chopped fresh dill**
- ☐ **12 pitted black olives, sliced**
- ☐ **2 tablespoons capers, finely chopped**
- ☐ **2-3 drops red pepper seasoning**
- ☐ **3 tablespoons cream**
- ☐ **2 tablespoons lemon juice**
- ☐ **freshly ground black pepper**

1   Melt butter in a saucepan, add flour and cook for 1 minute. Remove from heat.
2   Blend in milk, stock or broth and tuna liquid, stirring over a medium heat until sauce boils and thickens.
3   Reduce heat and add dill, olives, capers, red pepper seasoning, cream and lemon juice. Season to taste with pepper and stir well to combine.
4   Break up tuna into smaller chunks and fold through sauce. Cook for 2-3 minutes to heat through. Spoon sauce over hot, cooked pasta and serve.

## PASTA WITH MUSHROOM AND BACON SAUCE

*A rich creamy sauce that can be made in minutes. This sauce is best to use with the long varieties of pasta such as fettuccine, tagliarini, spaghetti or linguine.*

Serves 4

- ☐ **1 small head broccoli, cut into small florets**
- ☐ **2 teaspoons olive oil**
- ☐ **4 slices bacon, chopped**
- ☐ **4 oz (125 g) button mushrooms, sliced**
- ☐ **1 clove garlic, crushed**
- ☐ **1¹/₄ cups (300 mL) cream**
- ☐ **freshly ground black pepper**
- ☐ **3 tablespoons finely chopped fresh parsley**

1   Boil, steam or microwave broccoli until just tender. Drain and refresh under cold running water. Drain and set aside.
2   Heat oil in a skillet and cook bacon for 3-4 minutes or until crisp. Stir in mushrooms and garlic and cook for 2-3 minutes.
3   Pour in cream, bring to the boil, stirring frequently and simmer for 5 minutes or until sauce thickens. Season to taste with pepper, add broccoli and heat through. Spoon sauce over hot, cooked pasta. Sprinkle with parsley and serve.

*Seafood and Tomato Sauce, Tuna and Olive Sauce, Pasta with Mushroom and Bacon Sauce*

### PASTA PERFECTION

The success to perfect pasta is in the cooking.

✧   For perfect results every time, allow approximately 4 quarts (4 litres) of water to 1 pound (500 g) of pasta and use a very large saucepan. Bring the water to a rapid boil, add a dash of oil and a pinch of salt. The oil prevents the pasta sticking and the salt helps bring out the flavor. Add the pasta, give a stir and cook for the required time.

✧   Pasta is cooked when it is "al dente" (to the tooth tender but some resistance to the bite). It should not be overcooked and mushy.

✧   Cooking time varies, depending on the type of pasta you are cooking. Commercially packaged, dried pasta takes 10-12 minutes to cook, while fresh pasta takes 3-5 minutes. Once cooked, drain in a colander and rinse under cold water if the pasta is to be used as a cold dish. If it is to be served hot, stir through a little oil or melted butter to prevent the pasta sticking.

❖

## EGGPLANT AND RICE PIE

*A very tasty adaptation of the ever popular recipe, moussaka.*

Serves 6

- ☐ **2 large eggplants, cut into $^1/_4$-inch ($^1/_2$ cm) slices**
- ☐ **$^1/_2$ cup (125 mL) olive oil**
- ☐ **1 onion, chopped**
- ☐ **2 cloves garlic, crushed**
- ☐ **16 oz (500 g) lean ground beef**
- ☐ **14 oz (440 g) canned tomatoes, undrained and mashed**
- ☐ **1 tablespoon finely chopped fresh oregano**
- ☐ **2 tablespoons tomato paste**
- ☐ **freshly ground black pepper**
- ☐ **1 cup (175 g) brown rice, cooked**
- ☐ **1 cup (250 g) fresh or frozen peas, cooked**
- ☐ **$^3/_4$ cup (90 g) shredded Cheddar cheese**
- ☐ **3 tablespoons grated Parmesan cheese**
- ☐ **4 tablespoons dry bread crumbs**

*Eggplant and Rice Pie,*
*Cheese Baked Rice Custard*

1 Brush eggplant with oil. Heat half the remaining oil in a skillet. Place a single layer of eggplant in pan and cook until golden on each side. Remove and drain on paper towels. Repeat with remaining eggplant.

2 Heat remaining oil in pan and cook onion and garlic for 2-3 minutes or until onion softens. Stir in meat and cook for 6-8 minutes, or until meat browns.

3 Combine tomatoes, oregano, tomato paste and pepper to taste. Pour into pan. Simmer for 8-10 minutes, or until liquid reduces by half. Remove pan from heat and add rice, peas, Cheddar and Parmesan cheeses.

4 Grease a deep 9-inch (23 cm), round cake pan. Sprinkle half the bread crumbs over base and sides of pan. Place a layer of overlapping eggplant slices over base and side of pan. Spoon meat mixture over eggplant. Pack down well using the back of a spoon.

5 Overlap remaining eggplant slices over filling. Sprinkle with remaining bread crumbs. Bake at 350°F (180°C) for 25-30 minutes or until golden brown. Stand 5 minutes before turning out and serving.

## *Just right rice*

Wash rice before cooking to remove any loose starch and prevent the grains sticking during cooking. Wash rice in a large sieve under cold running water until the water running through the sieve is clear. Brown rice sometimes contains bits of husks; remove these by placing the rice in a bowl of water and any foreign bodies will float to the surface. There are several methods of cooking rice.

**Absorption method:** This is an easy way to cook rice, and the grains stay separate and fluffy. Brown and white rice can be cooked in this way. Bring 2 cups (500 mL) of water to boil in a heavy-based saucepan. Slowly add 1 cup of rice and salt to taste and return to the boil. Stir once, cover, then reduce heat to as low as possible. Simmer gently; 20-25 minutes for white and quick-cooking brown rice, 50-55 minutes for brown rice. At the end of cooking time the rice should be tender and all the liquid absorbed. Remove cover. Fork lightly and allow the steam to escape for about 5 minutes before serving. To cook larger quantities of rice by this method, increase the liquid by 1 cup (250 mL) to every extra cup (210 g) of rice.

**Rapid boil method:** Bring 2 quarts (2 litres) water to boil in a large saucepan and add salt to taste. Slowly add 1 cup (210 g) rice and boil rapidly; 12-15 minutes for white and quick-cooking brown rice and 30-40 minutes for brown, or until tender. Stir frequently during cooking.

**Steamed method:** Steaming is a popular Chinese method of cooking rice. Using this method the grains stay separate and fluffy. After washing 1 cup (210 g) rice, leave to drain and dry, then place in a heavy-based saucepan. Add enough water to cover the rice by 1 inch (2.5 cm). Bring to the boil and boil rapidly until steam holes (tunnels) appear on the surface of the rice. Reduce heat to as low as possible. Cover with a tight fitting lid, or foil, and steam; 10 minutes for white and quick-cooking brown rice, and 25-30 minutes for brown, or until tender. Remove lid, fork lightly and stand 5 minutes before serving.

**Microwave method:** Place 1 cup (210 g) washed rice in a large, deep microwave-safe bowl. Add $1^1/_2$ cups (375 mL) boiling water. Cover with lid or plastic food wrap and cook on HIGH (100%) for 10-13 minutes for white and quick-cooking brown rice. Stir once during cooking. Stand covered for 5 minutes before serving. If cooking brown rice, increase the quantity of water to 3 cups (750 mL) and allow 30 minutes for cooking.

## LASAGNE

Serves 6

- ☐ **9 sheets instant lasagne pasta**
- ☐ **¹/₂ cup (60 g) shredded mozzarella**
- ☐ **2 tablespoons grated Parmesan cheese**

MEAT SAUCE
- ☐ **2 teaspoons olive oil**
- ☐ **1 onion, chopped**
- ☐ **2 cloves garlic, crushed**
- ☐ **2 strips bacon, chopped**
- ☐ **4 oz (125 g) button mushrooms, sliced**
- ☐ **1 pound (500 g) lean ground beef**
- ☐ **14 oz (440 g) canned tomatoes, undrained and mashed**
- ☐ **¹/₂ cup (125 mL) red wine**
- ☐ **¹/₂ teaspoon dried basil**
- ☐ **¹/₂ teaspoon dried oregano**
- ☐ **1 teaspoon sugar**

SPINACH CHEESE SAUCE
- ☐ **2 tablespoons (30 g) butter**
- ☐ **2 tablespoons all-purpose flour**
- ☐ **1 cup (250 mL) milk**
- ☐ **¹/₂ cup (125 mL) cream**
- ☐ **¹/₂ cup (60 g) shredded mozzarella**
- ☐ **8 oz (250 g) package frozen spinach, thawed and drained**
- ☐ **freshly ground black pepper**

1   To make meat sauce, heat oil in a skillet and cook onion, garlic, bacon and mushrooms for 2-3 minutes, or until onion softens.

2   Add meat to pan and cook for 4-5 minutes, or until meat browns. Combine tomatoes, wine, basil, oregano and sugar and pour into pan with meat mixture and bring to the boil. Reduce heat, cover and simmer for 35 minutes, or until sauce thickens.

3   To make sauce, melt butter in a saucepan, add flour and cook for 1-2 minutes. Remove pan from heat and stir in milk and cream. Cook over medium heat, stirring continuously, until sauce boils and thickens.

4   Remove pan from heat and stir in cheese and spinach. Season with pepper.

5   To assemble lasagne, spread one-third of cheese sauce over base of a lightly greased 7 x 11-inch (18 x 28 cm) shallow baking dish. Top with three lasagne sheets, spread half the meat sauce over, then another third of spinach cheese sauce. Top with another three lasagne sheets and remaining meat sauce. Place remaining lasagne sheets over meat sauce and top with remaining cheese sauce.

6   Combine mozzarella and Parmesan cheeses and sprinkle over lasagne. Bake at 375°F (190°C) for 40 minutes or until golden.

## CHEESE BAKED RICE CUSTARD

*A baked rice custard with a difference – it has a surprise savory flavor rather than sweet.*

Serves 4

- ☐ **2 tablespoons (30 g) butter**
- ☐ **2 leeks, washed and sliced**
- ☐ **3 strips bacon, chopped**
- ☐ **¹/₂ red pepper, finely chopped**
- ☐ **¹/₄ cup (55 g) short grain rice, cooked**
- ☐ **1¹/₂ cups (375 mL) milk**
- ☐ **2 eggs, lightly beaten**
- ☐ **¹/₂ teaspoon dry mustard**
- ☐ **1 teaspoon Worcestershire sauce**
- ☐ **1 tablespoon mayonnaise**
- ☐ **1 cup (125 g) shredded Cheddar cheese**
- ☐ **2 tablespoons finely chopped fresh parsley**
- ☐ **1 teaspoon paprika**

1   Melt butter in a skillet. Cook leeks, bacon and pepper for 4-5 minutes, or until leeks soften and bacon browns. Remove pan from heat and stir rice through. Transfer rice mixture to a deep 1¹/₂-quart (1.5 litre) baking dish.

2   Place milk in a saucepan and bring almost to the boil. Remove pan from heat and whisk in eggs, mustard, Worcestershire sauce, mayonnaise, cheese and parsley. Pour milk mixture over rice mixture. Sprinkle lightly with paprika.

3   Place ovenproof dish in a baking pan. Fill baking pan with hot water, so it comes halfway up the side of the baking dish. Bake at 350°F (180°C) for 25-30 minutes, or until firm.

---

**COOK'S TIPS**

✧ If you are using fresh pasta, separate the strands before cooking. When the water returns to the boil, start the cooking time, maintaining a slow rolling boil. Stir just enough to separate the strands, or the pasta will release an excess of starch, which may cause sticking.

✧ As a recommended guideline, allow 3 oz (100 g) per person of dried pasta for a main meal, or 2 oz (60-70 g) for a first course. Allow 5 oz (150 g) of fresh pasta for a main meal and 3 oz (80-100 g) for a first course.

---

*Lasagne*

## RAINBOW RISOTTO

*This savory rice dish is enhanced by succulent pieces of colorful crisp vegetables.*

Serves 4

- [ ] 1 tablespoon vegetable oil
- [ ] 2 tablespoons (30 g) butter
- [ ] 1 onion, chopped
- [ ] $1/4$ teaspoon ground turmeric
- [ ] 2 cups (440 g) long grain rice
- [ ] 4 cups (1 liter) vegetable stock or broth
- [ ] 1 small butternut squash, peeled, seeded and chopped
- [ ] 4 oz (125 g) fresh or frozen peas
- [ ] 1 small red pepper, chopped
- [ ] 2 zucchini, chopped

1   Heat oil and butter in a large saucepan and cook onion and turmeric for 2-3 minutes. Stir in rice and stock or broth and bring to a boil. Reduce heat, cover and simmer for 15 minutes.

2   Boil, steam or microwave butternut squash and peas separately until tender. Drain and add to rice mixture with red pepper and zucchini. Cook for 4-5 minutes or until heated through.

❖

## RICE WITH MOZZARELLA AND HERBS

*Much simpler than a risotto, this dish relies on the quality of the fresh herbs and mozzarella used.*

Serves 4

- [ ] 16 cups (4 liters) water
- [ ] $1^1/2$ cups (315 g) Arborio rice
- [ ] $1/3$ cup (3 oz/90 g) butter, cut into small pieces
- [ ] 2 tablespoons chopped mixed fresh herbs
- [ ] 2 cups (250 g) shredded mozzarella cheese
- [ ] $1/4$ cup (60 g) grated fresh Parmesan cheese
- [ ] freshly ground black pepper

1   Place water in a large saucepan and bring to a boil. Add rice and cook, covered, for 15-20 minutes or until the rice is just tender. Stir occasionally during cooking to prevent sticking.

2   Drain, then return rice to same pan. Stir in butter and chopped herbs. Fold in mozzarella and Parmesan cheeses and season to taste with pepper. Transfer to a warm serving dish and serve immediately.

## SPAGHETTI WITH TUNA AND TOMATO SAUCE

Serves 4

- [ ] 1 pound (500 g) tubular spaghetti

TUNA SAUCE
- [ ] 14 oz (440 g) canned tuna in oil, drained and oil reserved
- [ ] 1 large onion, chopped
- [ ] 1 green pepper, sliced
- [ ] 1 teaspoon minced garlic
- [ ] 12 oz (375 g) tomato purée
- [ ] $1/2$ cup (125 mL) white wine
- [ ] 1 tablespoon cracked black pepper
- [ ] 2 tablespoons finely chopped fresh parsley
- [ ] 8 pitted black olives, halved

1   Cook spaghetti in boiling water in a large saucepan following packet directions. Drain, set aside and keep warm.

2   To make sauce, heat reserved oil from tuna in a skillet and cook onion, green pepper and garlic for 3-4 minutes or until onion is soft. Stir in tomato purée and wine and cook for 3-4 minutes.

3   Add tuna to sauce and cook, stirring gently, for 4-5 minutes. Spoon sauce over spaghetti and toss to combine. Garnish with black pepper, parsley and olives.

❖

## FETTUCCINE CARBONARA

Serves 4

- [ ] 1 pound (500 g) fettuccine
- [ ] 1 tablespoon olive oil

CARBONARA SAUCE
- [ ] 4 eggs
- [ ] 3 tablespoons thick cream
- [ ] 3 tablespoons grated Parmesan cheese
- [ ] freshly ground black pepper
- [ ] 4 slices bacon, chopped

1   Cook fettuccine in boiling water in a large saucepan following packet directions. Drain, then toss with 2 teaspoons oil. Set aside and keep warm.

2   To make sauce, place eggs, cream and Parmesan cheese in a mixing bowl and beat well to combine. Season to taste with black pepper.

3   Heat remaining oil in a large skillet and cook bacon for 4-5 minutes or until crisp. Add fettuccine and toss well. Pour egg mixture into pan and toss over a low heat for 1 minute or until egg is almost cooked. Remove from heat and serve immediately.

## TAGLIATELLE WITH SPINACH AND MUSHROOMS

Serves 4

- [ ] 1 pound (500 g) tagliatelle
- [ ] $1/4$ cup ($1/2$ stick/60 g) butter
- [ ] 1 clove garlic, crushed
- [ ] 2 tablespoons Marsala or dry sherry
- [ ] 8 oz (250 g) button mushrooms, sliced
- [ ] $1/2$ cup (250 mL) thick cream
- [ ] freshly ground black pepper
- [ ] $1^1/2$ pounds (750 g) fresh spinach, stalks removed and leaves shredded
- [ ] grated fresh Parmesan cheese

1   Cook tagliatelle in boiling water in a large saucepan following packet directions. Drain, set aside and keep warm.

2   Melt butter in a saucepan and cook garlic and Marsala or sherry over a low heat for 3 minutes or until mixture is syrupy. Add mushrooms and cook for 3 minutes longer. Blend in cream and bring to a boil. Season to taste with black pepper.

3   Add pasta to sauce. Toss in spinach and stir to coat. Cook over a low heat for 2-3 minutes, or until spinach is warmed through. Serve with Parmesan cheese.

❖

## RICOTTA AND HERB SAUCE

Serves 4

- [ ] 1 egg yolk
- [ ] $2/3$ cup (155 g) ricotta cheese
- [ ] $1/3$ cup (90 mL) thick cream
- [ ] 4 tablespoons grated fresh Parmesan cheese
- [ ] 1 teaspoon finely snipped fresh chives
- [ ] 1 teaspoon finely chopped fresh parsley
- [ ] coarsely ground white pepper

1   Beat egg yolk into ricotta cheese and mix until smooth. Set aside.

2   Heat cream in a saucepan, stir in Parmesan cheese, chives and parsley. Season to taste with white pepper. Beat through ricotta mixture just before serving. Spoon sauce over cooked pasta.

*Spaghetti with Tuna and Tomato*

## THREE-CHEESE SAUCE WITH PISTACHIOS

Serves 4

- ☐ **1 cup (250 mL) light cream**
- ☐ **¹/₃ cup (90 g) blue cheese, crumbled**
- ☐ **¹/₄ cup (60 g) grated fresh Parmesan cheese**
- ☐ **¹/₄ cup (60 g) grated fresh Romano cheese**
- ☐ **¹/₄ cup (60 g) shelled pistachio nuts, chopped**
- ☐ **1 teaspoon finely chopped fresh basil**
- ☐ **ground white pepper**

Place cream in a saucepan and bring to a boil. Reduce heat, add blue cheese and stir until smooth. Stir in Parmesan and Romano cheeses. Cook over a low heat, stirring constantly, until sauce is thick. Add pistachio nuts and basil. Season to taste with pepper. Spoon sauce over cooked pasta of your choice.

## MUSSEL, TOMATO AND ORANGE SAUCE

Serves 4

- ☐ **3 x 14 oz (440 g) canned tomatoes, drained**
- ☐ **1¹/₂ tablespoons olive oil**
- ☐ **1 onion, chopped**
- ☐ **1 clove garlic, crushed**
- ☐ **¹/₂ teaspoon dried chili flakes**
- ☐ **³/₄ cup (185 mL) dry white wine**
- ☐ **3 teaspoons finely chopped fresh oregano, or 1 teaspoon dried oregano**
- ☐ **¹/₂ teaspoon sugar**
- ☐ **3 tablespoons orange juice**
- ☐ **freshly ground black pepper**
- ☐ **16 mussels, cleaned and scrubbed**
- ☐ **2 teaspoons grated orange rind**
- ☐ **2 tablespoons finely chopped fresh parsley**

1 Squeeze tomatoes to push out seeds, pulping flesh as you go.

2 Heat oil in a large saucepan and cook onion, garlic and chili flakes for 5 minutes. Mix in tomatoes, ¹/₃ cup (100 mL) wine, oregano, sugar and orange juice. Season to taste with pepper. Bring to a boil, then reduce heat and simmer for 40 minutes, or until sauce reduces and thickens.

3 Place mussels in a baking dish and pour in remaining wine. Bake at 425°F (220°C) for 8-10 minutes or until mussels open. Discard any unopened mussels.

4 Combine orange rind and parsley. Add mussels to sauce, toss to coat and sprinkle with parsley mixture.

# Christmas dinner for ten

To make Christmas a celebration for all – including the cook – to enjoy, follow the valuable advice below on everything from planning, to making the cake, the pudding and cooking the turkey.

❖

## STUFFED TURKEY FILLETS

*We have chosen a boneless turkey breast fillet, but you might like to use the traditional whole turkey. You can mix and match the stuffings and sauces to suit your taste. The stuffings are suitable to use with pork, turkey, duck or chicken.*

Serves 10

- ☐ **2 x 2-pound (1 kg) boneless turkey breasts**
- ☐ **$^1/_2$ cup (125 mL) water**
- ☐ **2 tablespoons polyunsaturated oil**

1  Lay turkey breasts out flat, skin side down on a large board. Using a sharp knife, cut the breasts horizontally, almost all the way through the center. Open out breasts and place between two sheets of plastic food wrap. Pound lightly with a rolling pin to flatten slightly. Overlap breasts slightly to form one large roll.

2  Place stuffing of your choice down the center of turkey. Roll up to enclose stuffing and secure with wooden picks or tie with string at even intervals.

3  Place on a rack in a roasting pan. Pour water into the roasting pan and brush turkey with oil. Cover and bake at 350°F (180°C) for 1$^1/_4$ hours or until tender and cooked through. Stand covered for 15 minutes before slicing. Serve with sauce of your choice.

---

### STUFFINGS

✧  Any one of these stuffings can be used as described above or used to stuff a whole turkey.

✧  Stuffings can also be cooked separately. You might like to make and serve two or three stuffings.

---

❖

## PESTO STUFFING

- ☐ **3 cups (180 g) soft white bread crumbs**
- ☐ **5 tablespoons (80 g) butter, melted**
- ☐ **1 egg, lightly beaten**
- ☐ **3 cloves garlic, crushed**
- ☐ **$^1/_2$ cup (60 g) grated Parmesan cheese**
- ☐ **2 tablespoons finely chopped fresh basil**
- ☐ **$^1/_2$ cup (60 g) pine nuts, toasted**

Place bread crumbs, butter, egg, garlic, Parmesan cheese, basil and pine nuts in a bowl. Mix well to combine all ingredients.

❖

## RAISIN, APPLE AND GINGER STUFFING

- ☐ **3 cups (180 g) soft white bread crumbs**
- ☐ **5 tablespoons (80 g) butter, melted**
- ☐ **1 egg, lightly beaten**
- ☐ **$^1/_2$ cup (35 g) roughly chopped dried apple**
- ☐ **3 tablespoons raisins, chopped**
- ☐ **2 tablespoons grated fresh ginger**
- ☐ **2 tablespoons honey**
- ☐ **$^1/_4$ teaspoon ground cinnamon**
- ☐ **4 oz (120 g) ground pork**

Place bread crumbs, butter, egg, apple, raisins, ginger, honey, cinnamon and pork in a bowl and mix well to combine.

*Christmas Pudding with Hard Butter Sauce, Fruit Mince Tarts, Stuffed Turkey Fillet, Ginger and Lime Sauce, Ham with Apple and Citrus Glaze, Spicy Syrup Christmas Cake*

China from Villeroy and Boch

## FIG AND PECAN STUFFING

- [ ] **2 teaspoons vegetable oil**
- [ ] **1 large onion, chopped**
- [ ] **3 cups (180 g) soft white bread crumbs**
- [ ] **5 tablespoons (80 g) butter, melted**
- [ ] **1 egg, lightly beaten**
- [ ] **2 stalks celery, finely sliced**
- [ ] **1/2 cup (165 g) chopped dried figs**
- [ ] **3/4 cup (90 g) pecan nuts, chopped**
- [ ] **2 tablespoons finely chopped fresh parsley**
- [ ] **2 teaspoons ground cardamom**
- [ ] **3 teaspoons ground coriander**
- [ ] **2 teaspoons ground ginger**
- [ ] **freshly ground black pepper**

1 Heat oil in a skillet and cook onion for 4-5 minutes or until golden.
2 Place bread crumbs, butter, egg, onion, celery, figs, pecans, parsley, cardamom, coriander, ginger and pepper in a bowl and mix well to combine.

## TOMATO SAUCE

- [ ] **1 red pepper, quartered**
- [ ] **2 tomatoes, peeled, seeded and chopped**
- [ ] **2 tablespoons (30 g) butter**
- [ ] **1 onion, finely chopped**
- [ ] **6 peppercorns**
- [ ] **1 small bay leaf**
- [ ] **1 1/2 tablespoons tomato paste**
- [ ] **1/2 cup (125 mL) chicken stock or broth**

1 Broil pepper until skin blisters and blackens. Allow to cool, then peel off skin.
2 Place pepper and tomatoes in a food processor or blender and process until smooth.
3 Melt butter in a skillet and cook onion for 2-3 minutes or until soft. Stir in tomato mixture, peppercorns, bay leaf, tomato paste and chicken stock or broth. Simmer for 20 minutes, or until sauce reduces and thickens.

## GINGER AND LIME SAUCE

- [ ] **1 tablespoon (15 g) butter**
- [ ] **3 cloves garlic, finely sliced**
- [ ] **2 teaspoons grated fresh ginger**
- [ ] **1 1/2 cups (375 mL) stock, made from strained pan juices and chicken broth**
- [ ] **4 tablespoons lime marmalade**
- [ ] **1/2 cup (125 mL) Madeira wine**
- [ ] **1 1/2 tablespoons cornstarch blended with 3 tablespoons water**

1 Melt butter in a saucepan and cook garlic and ginger for 1-2 minutes. Stir in stock and cook over medium heat until mixture boils. Reduce heat and simmer for 10 minutes.
2 Strain mixture to remove garlic and ginger, then return to pan. Add lime marmalade, Madeira and cornstarch mixture and cook over a medium heat, stirring frequently until sauce boils and thickens.

## GRAVY MADE USING PAN JUICES

- [ ] **1 1/2 tablespoons all-purpose flour**
- [ ] **1 1/2 cups (375 mL) chicken stock or broth**
- [ ] **1 teaspoon Worcestershire sauce**

1 Drain all but 2 tablespoons of juices from the roasting pan. Stir in flour and cook over a medium heat until browned.
2 Remove pan from heat and gradually blend in stock or broth and Worcestershire sauce. Return to heat and cook, stirring constantly until gravy boils and thickens. Strain gravy into a small saucepan and cover to prevent a skin forming. Reheat when required.

## RUM AND FRUIT GLAZE

- [ ] **1/3 cup (60 g) dried apricots**
- [ ] **1/3 cup (60 g) dried apples**
- [ ] **1/3 cup (60 g) raisins**
- [ ] **5 tablespoons freshly squeezed orange juice**
- [ ] **4 tablespoons dark rum**
- [ ] **1/2 cup (180 g) apricot jam, warmed and strained**
- [ ] **2 tablespoons brown sugar**
- [ ] **2 teaspoons dry mustard**
- [ ] **2 tablespoons honey**
- [ ] **1/3 cup (60 g) sour cherries or 1/3 cup (60 g) pitted tart canned cherries packed in water, drained**
- [ ] **1/3 cup (60 g) seedless green grapes**
- [ ] **2 kiwifruit, peeled and cut into 1/2-inch (1 cm) cubes**
- [ ] **1/3 cup (60 g) pecan nuts**

1 Place apricots, apples and raisins in a bowl and pour over orange juice and rum. Cover and set aside to macerate for one hour, or preferably overnight.
2 Combine apricot jam, brown sugar, mustard and honey. Spread half the mixture over the prepared ham. Drain dried fruit and arrange decoratively with cherries, grapes, kiwifruit and pecans on top. Spoon over remaining glaze.

## Glazing and storing the ham

A glazed ham makes a delicious and stunning centerpiece for your Christmas table. These glazes will have your guests gasping in admiration at your talents. You can use either of the following glazes for cooked ham on the bone or canned ham.
**Ham on the bone:** Remove the rind, using a sharp knife to ease it away from the fat layer. Trim fat, leaving a thin layer. Score the surface of the fat in a diamond pattern, using the point of a sharp knife. Cut just through the surface; do not cut the fat too deeply or it will spread apart during cooking. Prepare the glaze and spread half, thinly, over the ham. Decorate with fruit and spoon over remaining glaze, taking care not to disturb the fruit arrangement. Place the ham into a lightly greased roasting pan and bake at 350°F (180°C) for 1-1 1/2 hours. Remove from oven and set aside to cool. Cover loosely with foil and store in the refrigerator until required.
**Canned ham:** Open the can at both ends, push ham out into a roasting pan. Bake at 350°F (180°C) for 5-10 minutes or until jelly melts. Drain jelly from pan, brush ham with glaze and decorate with fruit as for ham on the bone. Bake at 350°F (180°C) for 15-20 minutes.
**Storing ham on the bone:** After your Christmas dinner, you usually find yourself left with an abundance of ham. Leftover ham will keep for up to four weeks if stored correctly. Wrap the ham loosely in a clean wet tea towel or pillowcase and store in the refrigerator. Rinse and wring out the tea towel or pillowcase daily and replace around ham. Do not store ham in plastic or the original wrapper in which it was packaged.

## APPLE AND CITRUS GLAZE

- [ ] **1/2 cup (180 g) apricot jam, warmed and strained**
- [ ] **2 tablespoons brown sugar**
- [ ] **2 teaspoons honey**
- [ ] **2 green apples, peeled, cored, halved and thinly sliced**
- [ ] **2 oranges, peeled and thinly sliced**

Combine jam, sugar and honey; spread half the mixture over prepared ham. Arrange alternate slices of apple and orange on top, then spoon remaining glaze over.

## BASIC FRUIT MIXTURE

*This Basic Fruit Mixture is designed for those who wish to make the most of their time during the Christmas season. Make the mixture up to one month in advance and store it in an airtight container, in the refrigerator. Stir the fruit occasionally. In this recipe Midori liqueur (melon liqueur) has been used but you may like to use brandy or sweet sherry instead. This amount of mixture is sufficient to make a traditional English Christmas cake, a pudding and twenty-four mincemeat tartlets.*

- ☐ **2 pounds (1 kg) golden raisins, halved**
- ☐ **3 cups (375 g) currants**
- ☐ **1³/₄ cups (170 g) seeded raisins, chopped**
- ☐ **2 tablespoons (30 g) mixed candied peel, chopped**
- ☐ **1 cup (155 g) pitted dried dates, chopped into small pieces**
- ☐ **1 cup (170 g) dried apricots, chopped into small pieces**
- ☐ **1 cup (155 g) pitted prunes, chopped into small pieces**
- ☐ **2 cups (250 g) glacé (candied) cherries, quartered**
- ☐ **1 cup (155 g) glacé (candied) pineapple, chopped into small pieces**
- ☐ **¹/₂ honeydew melon, peeled, seeded and chopped**
- ☐ **¹/₄ cup (75 g) angelica, chopped**
- ☐ **1 cup (360 g) honey**
- ☐ **1 cup (250 mL) Midori liqueur**

Place golden raisins, currants, seeded raisins, mixed peel, dates, apricots, prunes, cherries, pineapple, honeydew and angelica in a large mixing bowl. Stir in honey and liqueur; mix well to combine. Cover tightly with plastic food wrap and stand overnight, or transfer to an airtight container and store in the refrigerator until required.

*Making a boiled Christmas Pudding*

## CHRISTMAS PUDDING

Serves 8

- ☐ **1 cup (2 sticks/250 g) butter, softened**
- ☐ **¹/₂ cup (60 g) couscous**
- ☐ **3 eggs, lightly beaten**
- ☐ **4 tablespoons honey**
- ☐ **2¹/₄ cups (135 g) soft rye bread crumbs**
- ☐ **2 cups (220 g) ground hazelnuts**
- ☐ **¹/₄ recipe Basic Fruit Mixture**

Cream butter until pale and creamy. Add couscous, eggs and honey and beat well. Fold in bread crumbs, ground nuts and the fruit mixture. Spoon mixture into 2-quart (8-cup) pudding mold or divide mixture between two 1-quart (4-cup) pudding molds. Steam for 2¹/₂ hours for small molds or 4 hours for large.

---

## SPICY SYRUP CHRISTMAS CAKE

Makes 1 cake

- ☐ **1 cup (2 sticks/250 g) butter**
- ☐ **2¹/₂ cups (425 g) medium to fine semolina**
- ☐ **5 eggs, lightly beaten**
- ☐ **1 cup (220 g) superfine sugar**
- ☐ **2 teaspoons mixed spice**
- ☐ **1 teaspoon grated orange rind**
- ☐ **¹/₂ recipe Basic Fruit Mixture**

SYRUP
- ☐ **1 orange**
- ☐ **1¹/₂ cups (375 mL) water**
- ☐ **1¹/₂ cups (375 g) granulated sugar**
- ☐ **1 cinnamon stick**

1   Place butter in a large mixing bowl and beat until light and creamy. Add semolina and beat in eggs one at a time, beating well after each addition.
2   Add superfine sugar a little at a time, beating well after each addition. Stir in spice, orange rind and fruit mixture. Mix well to combine. Spoon mixture into a 9-inch (23 cm) lined, square cake pan at least 3 inches (7.5 cm) deep. Bake at 325°F (160°C) for 2¹/₂-3 hours or until cooked.
3   To make syrup, cut two to three thin strips of rind only, from the orange, using a vegetable peeler. Place water, sugar, cinnamon stick and orange peel in a saucepan and cook over medium heat, stirring constantly until sugar dissolves. Bring syrup to the boil without stirring, then reduce heat and simmer for 10 minutes. Set aside to cool slightly, then strain.
4   Remove cake from oven. Pour syrup over and set aside to cool in cake pan.

---

---

## FRUIT MINCE TARTS

Makes 24

FILLING
- ☐ **2 tablespoons honey**
- ☐ **¹/₂ cup (1 stick/125 g) butter, frozen and shredded**
- ☐ **¹/₄ recipe Basic Fruit Mixture**

ALMOND PASTRY
- ☐ **2 cups (250 g) all-purpose flour**
- ☐ **¹/₂ cup (1 stick/125 g) butter, chilled and cut into small pieces**
- ☐ **³/₄ cup (165 g) superfine sugar**
- ☐ **¹/₂ cup (60 g) ground almonds**
- ☐ **3 drops almond extract**
- ☐ **2-3 tablespoons ice water**
- ☐ **confectioners' sugar for dusting**

1   To make filling, place honey, butter and fruit mixture in a mixing bowl. Mix lightly to combine and set aside.
2   To make pastry, sift flour into a large mixing bowl. Cut in butter with fingertips or two knives, until mixture resembles fine bread crumbs. Stir in sugar, almonds, extract and enough water to mix to a firm dough. Refrigerate for 30 minutes. Roll out pastry to ¹/₈-inch (3 mm) in thickness. Cut pastry into twenty-four 3-inch (7 cm) rounds and twenty-four 2-inch (5.5 cm) rounds, using metal pastry cutters. Place larger pastry rounds in lightly greased muffin pans. Spoon in filling and top with smaller pastry rounds. Press edges together and bake at 350°F (180°C) for 15-20 minutes or until pastry is golden and crisp. Stand in pans for 10 minutes before removing to a wire rack to cool. Serve warm, or at room temperature, dusted lightly with confectioners' sugar.

---

---

## HARD BUTTER SAUCE

*Make 3 months in advance and freeze.*

Makes 1¹/₂ cups (185 g)

- ☐ **¹/₂ cup (1 stick/125 g) butter, softened**
- ☐ **2 cups (350 g) confectioners' sugar, sifted**

Beat butter until pale and creamy. Add confectioners' sugar a little at a time, beating well after each addition until light and fluffy.

---

## PECAN AND LIQUEUR BUTTER SAUCE

- ☐ **1 recipe Hard Butter Sauce**
- ☐ **2 tablespoons whiskey cream liqueur**
- ☐ **3 tablespoons ground pecans**

1   Make up Hard Butter Sauce as above and fold through liqueur and nuts.
2   Spoon mixture into a piping bag fitted with a large star piping nozzle. Pipe rosettes onto a cookie sheet, covered with aluminum foil and freeze until required. Remove 30 minutes prior to serving.

---

## BRANDIED ORANGE BUTTER SAUCE

- ☐ **1 recipe Hard Butter Sauce**
- ☐ **1¹/₂ tablespoons brandy**
- ☐ **2 teaspoons grated orange rind**

1   Make up Hard Butter Sauce as for the basic recipe, then fold through brandy and orange rind.
2   Spoon mixture onto a large piece of aluminum foil. Form into a rectangular shape with a spatula. Enclose with foil and freeze until required. Remove from freezer 30 minutes prior to serving and cut into slices to serve.

---

## ALMOND LIQUEUR BUTTER SAUCE

- ☐ **1 recipe Hard Butter Sauce**
- ☐ **2 tablespoons Amaretto (almond liqueur)**

1   Make up Hard Butter Sauce as for the basic recipe, then fold through Amaretto.
2   Spoon mixture onto a large piece of aluminum foil. Form into a rectangular shape with a spatula. Enclose with foil and freeze until required. Remove from freezer 30 minutes prior to serving and cut into slices to serve.

Laminate from Albet Laminati

## Cooking the traditional English Christmas pudding

**Boiling the pudding:** First prepare the pudding cloth. Purchase half a yard (half a metre) of unbleached calico, cut in half and trim to give two square pudding cloths. Soak calico overnight in cold water, then boil for 20 minutes and rinse well. Dip the prepared cloth into boiling water and, using rubber gloves to protect hands, wring excess water from cloth. Spread cloth out over a work surface and sprinkle with 5 tablespoons all-purpose flour. Working quickly, rub flour into cloth, covering an area of about 15 inches (38 cm) in diameter. The flour should be thicker in the center of cloth. Spoon mixture into the center of the cloth, then gather up the ends of cloth firmly around the pudding. Mold pudding with hands to form a smooth round shape. Tie with string as close to pudding as possible. Make a loop in the string for ease in lifting the pudding in and out of water and for hanging it after cooking. To ensure that the pudding is as round as possible pull the ends of the cloth tightly. Fill a large kettle three-quarters with water and bring to the boil. Quickly, but gently, lower the pudding into the water, cover and boil rapidly for the required time. Add more boiling water as it evaporates. There must be enough water in the kettle at all times for the pudding to move freely and float. When the cooking is complete, remove pudding from the kettle using the handle of a wooden spoon placed through the string loop. Carefully lift out of the water. Suspend the pudding from a drawer or cupboard handle. It is important for the pudding to be able to swing freely without touching anything. Keep cloth ends away from pudding by twisting them around the supporting string. The cloth will start to dry out in patches within a few minutes. Allow the pudding to dry overnight or until completely cold, then take it down. Cut the string and loosen cloth from top of pudding. Remove any excess flour. Set aside at room temperature until top of cloth is completely dry – this could take a day or two. Retie pudding cloth and store pudding in an airtight container in the refrigerator until required. Remove the pudding from the refrigerator about twelve hours before it is to be reheated.

Boil the pudding for 1 hour and then suspend as before for 10 minutes. Cut the string and carefully remove the cloth to expose one-quarter of the pudding. Using a towel to protect your hands invert the pudding onto a serving plate, then slowly and carefully pull away the cloth. Leave the pudding to stand at room temperature for 20 minutes before cutting. The longer the pudding stands the darker the skin will become.

**Steaming the pudding:** Spoon the pudding mixture into a well-greased china or aluminum pudding basin. Cover with a large piece of greased aluminum foil. If basin has a lid, place the lid over the foil and bring surplus foil up over it. If the basin has no lid, tie the foil securely in position, using string. Lower pudding into a large kettle containing sufficient boiling water to come halfway up the side of the basin. Add more boiling water as required during cooking. On completion of cooking remove and set aside to cool to room temperature. Refrigerate in basin for up to six weeks. On the day of serving steam for 1 hour then turn out and serve.

*Spicy Syrup Christmas Cake*

# Chocolate making

Chocolate making is easy and lots of fun. It is an inexpensive way to make personalized gifts for your special friends or family. As with most skills, practice makes perfect.

## Melting chocolate

✧ Chocolate melts more rapidly if broken into small pieces.

✧ The melting process should occur slowly, as chocolate scorches if overheated.

✧ To melt chocolate, place it in the top of double-boiler and set aside. Fill the bottom part of double-boiler with enough water to come just under top pan; the water should not touch the top pan. Bring water to the boil, then remove from heat and place chocolate over the hot water. Stand off the heat, stirring occasionally until chocolate melts and is of a smooth consistency. Cool at room temperature.

✧ Chocolate can be melted quickly and easily in the microwave oven. Place chocolate in a microwave-safe dish and cook on HIGH (100%) for 2 minutes per 12 oz (400 g) chocolate. When melting chocolate in the microwave oven you will find that it tends to hold its shape, so always stir it before additional heating. If the chocolate is not completely melted, cook it for an extra 30 seconds, then stir again.

### CHOCOLATE SUBSTITUTES

Compound chocolate, also called chocolate coating, is designed to replace couverture chocolate for coating. It can be purchased in block form or as round disks. Both forms are available in milk or dark chocolate. Compound chocolate is made from a vegetable oil base with sugar, milk solids and flavoring. It contains cocoa powder, but not cocoa butter and is easy to melt; it does not require tempering and is the easiest form for beginners to work with.

## Storing chocolate

Chocolate should be stored in a dry, airy place at a temperature of about 60°F (16°C). If stored in unsuitable conditions, the cocoa butter in chocolate may rise to the surface, leaving a white film. A similar discoloration occurs when water condenses on the surface. This often happens to refrigerated chocolates that are too loosely wrapped. Chocolate affected this way is still suitable for melting, but not for grating.

## Molded chocolates

**Solid chocolates:** It is important to have the molds clean and dry. Fill the mold with melted chocolate and tap on a hard surface to remove any air bubbles. Place mold in the freezer for 3 minutes or until set. When set remove from freezer and tap mold gently to remove chocolates.

**Filled chocolates:** Quarter-fill the mold with melted chocolate and tap to remove any air bubbles. Brush the chocolate evenly up the sides of the mold to make a shell and freeze 2 minutes or until set. Add a filling such as fondant, fruit or liqueur. Fill the top with melted chocolate and tap to remove air bubbles. Return mold to the freezer for 3 minutes or until set. Remove from freezer and tap gently to remove. Larger chocolate cases to hold desserts can also be made in this way, using foil-lined individual metal tartlet pans, brioche or muffin pans as the molds. When set, remove from pans and fill with a dessert filling such as mousse or a flavored cream.

**Marbled chocolates:** Spoon a little melted, white and dark chocolate separately into a dish. Using a teaspoon, swirl the white chocolate into the dark chocolate to make a marble pattern, then proceed as above.

## Chocolate decorations

**Chocolate caraques:** Pour melted chocolate over a cool work surface such as marble, ceramic or granite. Spread the chocolate as smoothly as possible using a flexible metal spatula, in a layer about $1/16$-inch (1.5 mm) thick; do not leave any holes. If the chocolate is too thick it will not roll. Allow chocolate to set at room temperature. Holding a long sharp knife at a 45° angle, pull gently over the surface of the chocolate to form curls.

**Chocolate curls and shavings:** Chocolate curls are made from chocolate that is at room temperature. To make shavings, chill the chocolate first. Using a vegetable peeler, shave the sides of the chocolate. Curls or shavings will fall depending on the temperature of the chocolate.

**Chocolate leaves:** Use stiff, fresh, non-poisonous leaves such as rose or lemon leaves. Keep as much stem as possible to hold onto. Wash and dry leaves, brush the shiny surface of the leaf with a thin layer of melted, cooled chocolate. Allow to set to room temperature then carefully peel away leaf.

**Piping chocolate:** Chocolate can be piped into fancy shapes for decorating desserts or cakes. Trace a simple design on a thin piece of paper. Tape a sheet of parchment paper to the work surface and slide the drawing under the sheet of paper. Pipe over outline with melted chocolate. Allow to set at room temperature, then remove carefully with a metal spatula.

*Chocolate making is lots of fun*

# Take a scone dough

Who can resist the aroma of freshly baked biscuits? This section is filled with tempting recipes that will show you how versatile a baking powder biscuit dough can be.

❖

## BASIC BISCUITS

Makes 10

- ☐ **2 cups (250 g) sifted all-purpose flour**
- ☐ **4 teaspoons baking powder**
- ☐ **2 teaspoons sugar**
- ☐ **$^1/_2$ teaspoon salt**
- ☐ **$^1/_3$ cup (50 g) butter or shortening, chopped**
- ☐ **1 egg, lightly beaten**
- ☐ **$^1/_2$ to $^2/_3$ cup (125-170 mL) milk**

1  Sift dry ingredients together into a mixing bowl. Cut in butter, using a fork or pastry blender, until mixture resembles coarse bread crumbs.

2  Make a well in the center of the mix. Using a fork, mix the egg and almost all the milk through the flour. Mix to a soft dough, adding remaining milk if necessary.

3  Turn onto a lightly floured surface and knead lightly 10-12 strokes until smooth. Using heel of hand, press dough out evenly to $^3/_4$-inch (2 cm) thickness. Cut biscuits out using a floured 2-inch (5 cm) biscuit cutter; do not twist the cutter, or the biscuits will rise unevenly.

4  For crusty biscuits, arrange biscuits $^3/_4$-inch (2 cm) apart on a greased and lightly floured cookie sheet. Brush tops with a little milk and bake at 450°F (220°C) for 10-12 minutes or until biscuits are golden brown and sound hollow when tapped with your fingertips.

---

### PERFECT BISCUITS

✧  Work quickly and have all the equipment cool.

✧  If you wrap biscuits in a clean tea towel when cooked, they will be soft and light. If you leave biscuits on a cooling rack they form a hard crust.

✧  Use the Basic Biscuits recipe to make a quick and easy pizza base.

✧  You can freeze biscuits for up to 3 months in an airtight container or a sealed freezer bag.

---

❖

## ALMOND SPIRAL

Serves 10

- ☐ **1 recipe Basic Biscuits dough with 2 teaspoons mixed spice added to flour**
- ☐ **$^1/_2$ cup (125 g) almond paste**
- ☐ **$^1/_2$ cup (80 g) chopped unblanched almonds**

GLAZE
- ☐ **1 tablespoon water**
- ☐ **2 tablespoons sugar**
- ☐ **2 tablespoons honey**

1  Roll biscuit dough out on a lightly floured surface, to form a rectangle $^1/_2$-inch (1 cm) in thickness. Spread with almond paste and sprinkle with nuts. Roll up like a jelly roll, starting from the shorter end. Using a sharp knife, cut slits three-quarters of the way through the roll, 1 inch (2.5 cm) apart.

2  Place roll on a lightly greased and floured cookie sheet and shape into a horseshoe. Twist each slice upwards so that the filling shows. Bake at 450°F (220°C) for 15-20 minutes, or until golden brown and sounds hollow when tapped.

3  To make glaze, place water, sugar and honey in a small saucepan and heat, stirring constantly, until sugar dissolves and ingredients are well combined. Bring to the boil and simmer for 2 minutes. Remove from heat and brush over warm spiral.

Glassware from HAG

*Left: Basic Biscuits*
*Above Right: Pumpkin Damper, Apple Dumplings in Caramel Sauce, Pesto Pinwheels, Almond Spiral*

## "AUSSIE" PUMPKIN DAMPER

Serves 8

- ☐ **2 cups (250 g) self-rising flour**
- ☐ **1 teaspoon baking powder**
- ☐ **1 teaspoon ground mixed spice**
- ☐ **1 teaspoon ground nutmeg**
- ☐ **2 teaspoons sugar**
- ☐ **3 tablespoons (50 g) butter, chopped**
- ☐ **¹/₂ cup (100 g) chopped prunes**
- ☐ **1 cup mashed cooked and well drained, or canned, pumpkin**
- ☐ **3-4 tablespoons water**

1   Sift flour, baking powder, mixed spice and nutmeg together in a bowl. Add sugar. Rub in butter, until mixture resembles fine bread crumbs. Stir in prunes.

2   Make a well in the center of the flour and, using a round-ended knife, mix in the pumpkin and water. Mix to a soft dough.

3   Turn onto a lightly floured surface and knead dough lightly until smooth, then shape into a round about 7 inches (18 cm) in diameter. Place on a greased and lightly floured cookie sheet. Brush top lightly with milk and sprinkle with a little extra flour. Mark into eight wedges, using a sharp knife and bake at 425°F (220°C) for 10 minutes. Reduce heat to 350°F (180°C) and bake for 50 minutes, or until cooked.

## PESTO PINWHEELS

Makes 10

- ☐ **1 recipe Basic Biscuits dough**
- ☐ **2 tablespoons milk**
- ☐ **¹/₂ cup (60 g) shredded Cheddar cheese**

PESTO FILLING

- ☐ **1¹/₂ cups (90 g) loosely packed fresh basil leaves**
- ☐ **3 cloves garlic, crushed**
- ☐ **3 tablespoons pine nuts, toasted**
- ☐ **3 tablespoons olive oil**
- ☐ **3 tablespoons grated Parmesan cheese**
- ☐ **freshly ground black pepper**

1   To make filling, place basil, garlic, pine nuts and 2 tablespoons of oil in a food processor and process until combined. With machine running, gradually add remaining oil. Transfer to a small bowl, mix in cheese and season with pepper.

2   Roll out biscuit dough, on a lightly floured surface, to form a rectangle ¹/₂-inch (1 cm) in thickness. Spread with filling and roll up like a jelly roll. Cut roll into ³/₄-inch (2 cm) wide slices. Place slices on a lightly greased and floured cookie sheet, brush each with a little milk and sprinkle with cheese. Bake at 425°F (220°C) for 15-20 minutes, or until cooked.

## APPLE DUMPLINGS IN CARAMEL SAUCE

Serves 8

- ☐ **1 recipe Basic Biscuits dough**
- ☐ **2 apples, peeled, cored and each cut into eight wedges**

CARAMEL SAUCE

- ☐ **2 cups (340 g) packed brown sugar**
- ☐ **2 tablespoons honey**
- ☐ **2 cups water**
- ☐ **¹/₄ cup (¹/₂ stick/60 g) butter**
- ☐ **1 teaspoon vanilla extract**

1   Roll dough out to ¹/₄-inch (5 mm) thickness and cut into rounds using a floured 4-inch (9 cm) biscuit cutter. Place an apple wedge on one half of each round, brush rim with a little milk, fold over and seal by pinching with fingertips.

2   To make sauce, place sugar, honey, water, butter and vanilla in a saucepan and heat, stirring constantly, until sugar dissolves and butter melts. Bring to the boil and simmer for 2 minutes.

3   Transfer sauce to a shallow baking dish, drop dumplings in and bake at 350°F (180°C) for 35-40 minutes or until sauce thickens and dumplings are cooked through.

# Take a butter cake

Add interest to your cakes by cooking them in differently shaped pans. The following recipe works perfectly if you follow the cooking times given in the chart.

### ❖ BASIC BUTTER CAKE

- ☐ $^1/_2$ **cup (1 stick/125 g) butter**
- ☐ **1 teaspoon vanilla extract**
- ☐ $^3/_4$ **cup (185 g) superfine sugar**
- ☐ **2 eggs**
- ☐ **1$^1/_2$ cups (185 g) all-purpose flour, sifted**
- ☐ **1$^1/_2$ teaspoons baking powder**
- ☐ $^1/_2$ **cup (125 mL) milk**

1  Cream butter and vanilla in a small mixing bowl until light and fluffy. Add sugar gradually, beating well after each addition.
2  Beat in eggs one at a time. Combine flour and baking powder and fold in alternately with milk. Spoon mixture into prepared cake pan.
3  Bake according to size of cake pan you have chosen. Stand 5 minutes before turning out onto a wire rack to cool. When cool, ice with frosting of your choice.

## Variations

**Chocolate Cake:** Mix 2 oz (60 g) melted, cooled baking chocolate into the basic cake mixture before adding flour and milk. Bake according to pan size. Stand 5 minutes before turning out.

**Apple Cake:** Spread two-thirds of the cake mixture into the prepared cake pan. Top with $^1/_2$ cup (200 g) canned apple pie filling, then remaining cake mixture. Bake according to cake pan size. Stand 10 minutes before turning out.

**Orange Cake:** Replace vanilla with 2 teaspoons grated orange rind when creaming butter. Substitute orange juice for milk. Bake according to cake pan size. Stand 5 minutes before turning out.

**Coffee Cake:** Replace vanilla with 1 tablespoon instant coffee dissolved in 1 tablespoon boiling water. Cool then cream with butter. Bake according to cake pan size. Stand 5 minutes before turning out.

**Coconut Cake:** Replace vanilla with $^1/_2$ teaspoon coconut extract and add $^1/_2$ cup (45 g) flaked or shredded coconut with flour and baking powder. Bake according to pan size. Stand 5 minutes then turn out.

**Banana Cake:** Omit milk and add 3 small very ripe mashed bananas to creamed butter and egg mixture. Combine flour, baking powder and 1 teaspoon baking soda, and fold into butter and egg mixture. Bake according to pan size. Stand 5 minutes before turning out.

### ❖ LEMON CREAM CHEESE FROSTING

- ☐ $^1/_2$ **cup (125 g) cream cheese, softened**
- ☐ **1 teaspoon grated lemon rind**
- ☐ **1$^1/_2$ cups (250 g) confectioners' sugar, sifted**
- ☐ **2 teaspoons lemon juice**

Beat cream cheese in a small mixing bowl until creamy. Add lemon rind, confectioners' sugar and lemon juice and mix well. Use as desired.

## ❖ CHOCOLATE FROSTING

- ☐ **6 tablespoons ($^3/_4$ stick/90 g) butter**
- ☐ **1$^1/_2$ cups (250 g) confectioners' sugar, sifted**
- ☐ **1 tablespoon cocoa, sifted**
- ☐ **2 tablespoons cream**

Beat butter in a small bowl until creamy. Add confectioners' sugar, cocoa and cream. Beat until frosting is a spreading consistency. Use as desired.

## ❖ ORANGE CREAM FROSTING

- ☐ **$^1/_4$ cup (60 g) cream cheese, softened**
- ☐ **2 tablespoons cream**
- ☐ **1 teaspoon grated orange rind**
- ☐ **1$^1/_2$ cups (250 g) confectioners' sugar, sifted**

Beat cream cheese, cream and orange rind in a small mixing bowl until creamy. Add confectioners' sugar and beat until smooth. Use as desired.

## PREPARATION AND COOKING TIMES

| PAN SIZE | PREPARATION | TEMPERATURE | COOKING TIME |
|---|---|---|---|
| 8-inch (20 cm) ring pan | Grease and paper-line | 350°F (180°C) | 40 mins |
| 8-inch (20 cm) round pan, 3-4 inches (7.5-10 cm) deep | Grease and paper-line | 350°F (180°C) | 50 mins |
| 8-inch (20 cm) baba kugelhopf pan | Lightly greased | 350°F (180°C) | 40 mins |
| 5 x 9-inch (14 x 21 cm) loaf pan | Grease and paper-line | 350°F (180°C) | 60 mins |
| 24 small (or miniature) cupcake pans | Paper cupcake liners | 400°F (200°C) | 15 mins |

Note: The cooking times in this chart are approximate and may vary depending on your oven. Always check your cake 5-10 minutes before the cooking time indicated in the recipe.

## ❖
## CHOCOLATE CELEBRATION CAKE

*This easy gâteau is sure to impress. For added effect you might like to decorate the top with chocolate curls, caraques or chocolate leaves. See page 71 for how to make these.*

- ☐ $3/4$ cup (90 g) unsweetened cocoa, sifted
- ☐ $1^1/2$ cups (375 mL) boiling water
- ☐ $3/4$ cup ($1^1/2$ sticks/185 g) butter
- ☐ $1^3/4$ cups (385 g) superfine sugar
- ☐ 2 tablespoons cherry conserve
- ☐ 3 eggs
- ☐ $2^1/4$ cups (310 g) self-rising flour, sifted
- ☐ 1 cup (100 g) toasted sliced almonds, chopped

CHERRY FILLING
- ☐ 3 tablespoons cherry jam
- ☐ $1/2$ cup (110 g) confectioners' sugar
- ☐ 3 tablespoons ground almonds
- ☐ 2 teaspoons Kirsch

COFFEE FROSTING
- ☐ $1/4$ cup ($1/2$ stick/60 g) butter
- ☐ $2^1/2$ cups (250 g) confectioners' sugar, sifted
- ☐ 2 teaspoons instant coffee, dissolved in 1 tablespoon boiling water

1   Combine cocoa and boiling water. Mix to dissolve. Set aside to cool completely.
2   Cream butter, sugar and jam until light and fluffy. Beat in eggs one at a time, adding a little flour with each egg. Fold in remaining flour and cocoa mixture, alternately.
3   Spoon mixture into two greased and lined 8-inch (20 cm) cake pans. Bake at 350°F (180°C) for 35 minutes, or until cooked when tested with a skewer. Cool in pan for 5 minutes before turning out onto a wire rack to cool completely.
4   To make filling, place conserve, confectioners' sugar, almonds and Kirsch in a bowl. Mix well until combined.
5   To make frosting, beat butter in a small mixing bowl until creamy. Add confectioners' sugar and cooled coffee mixture and beat until frosting is of spreading consistency. Place one cake layer on a serving plate and spread with filling. Top with remaining cake layer and spread frosting over top and side of cake. Press almonds onto side of cake and decorate top with chocolate caraques or leaves.

*Chocolate Celebration Cake*

# Take a biscuit

A quick and easy cookie recipe is always an asset. It's ideal for lunchboxes, after-school treats, or a coffee break with unexpected guests.

*Glass Cake Stands from HAG*

## BASIC COOKIES

Makes 40

- ☐ ¹/₂ **cup (1 stick/125 g) butter**
- ☐ ³/₄ **cup (185 g) superfine sugar**
- ☐ **1 teaspoon vanilla extract**
- ☐ **1 egg**
- ☐ **1 cup (125 g) all-purpose flour, sifted**
- ☐ **1 cup (125 g) self-rising flour, sifted**

1   Cream butter, sugar and vanilla until light and fluffy. Add egg and beat well. Fold in all-purpose and self-rising flours, cover and refrigerate for 2 hours.
2   Roll heaped teaspoonfuls of mixture into balls. Place onto a greased cookie sheet, spacing well apart to allow for spreading. Flatten each ball slightly with a fork and bake at 350°F (180°C) for 12-15 minutes or until golden brown. Allow to cool on cookie sheet for a few minutes then transfer to a wire rack to finish cooling.

### Variations

**Spicy Fruit Cookies:** Replace 4 tablespoons of the superfine sugar with 4 tablespoons brown sugar. Sift 2 teaspoons of cinnamon, 1 teaspoon of mixed spice and 1 teaspoon of ginger with the flour. Roll out mixture and cut 16 rounds with a cookie cutter. Place teaspoonfuls of fruit mincemeat on half the rounds and cover with remaining rounds. Press the edges lightly to seal and bake at 350°F (180°C) for 20-25 minutes, or until golden brown.
**Three-Chocolate Cookies:** Add 1¹/₂ oz (40 g) finely chopped dark chocolate, 1¹/₂ oz (40 g) finely chopped milk chocolate and 1¹/₂ oz (40 g) finely chopped white chocolate to the mixture after beating in the egg. Place spoonfuls of mixture on a greased cookie sheet and bake at 350°F (180°C) for 12-15 minutes or until golden brown.
**Creamy Jam Drops:** Roll mixture into balls and flatten slightly. Make indents in the center of each round and fill with a small amount of cream cheese and top with a teaspoon of blackberry jam, or a jam of your choice. Be careful not to fill the holes too much, or the jam will overflow during cooking. Bake at 350°F (180°C) for 12-15 minutes, or until golden brown.

*Basic Cookies, Spicy Fruit Cookies, Three-Chocolate Cookies, Creamy Jam Drops, Date Wraps*

### DATE WRAPS

Makes 20

- ☐ **20 dried dates, pitted**
- ☐ **4 tablespoons brandy**
- ☐ **1 recipe Basic Cookies**

1   Soak dates in brandy for 30 minutes, then drain.
2   Divide cookie dough into 20 equal portions. Mold each portion around a date. Place on a greased cookie sheet and bake at 325°F (160°C) for 20-25 minutes, or until golden brown.

# Take some pastry

## RICH SHORTCRUST PASTRY

Makes a 9-inch (23 cm) pie crust

- ☐ **2 cups (250 g) all-purpose flour, sifted**
- ☐ **³/4 cup (1¹/2 sticks/185 g) butter, chilled and cut into small cubes**
- ☐ **1 egg yolk, lightly beaten**
- ☐ **3-4 tablespoons water, chilled**

1  Place flour into a medium bowl and rub in butter with fingertips until the mixture resembles bread crumbs.
2  Mix in egg yolk and enough water to form a soft dough with a metal spatula or round-ended knife.
3  Turn onto a lightly floured surface and knead gently until smooth. Wrap in plastic wrap and refrigerate for 30 minutes. Roll and use as desired.

### BAKING BLIND

✧  To bake blind means to precook the pastry shell without the filling. This is done when the filling you are using requires little or no cooking.
✧  To bake blind, line the pastry shell with waxed paper, a double layer of kitchen paper, or foil. Place uncooked rice or dried beans on the paper to weigh down the pastry, as this prevents it from rising during cooking. Make sure that you push the rice or beans right to the sides, to support them. Bake as directed.

*Butterscotch, Apple and Date Tart, Apple and Lemon Tartlets*

## BUTTERSCOTCH, APPLE AND DATE TART

Serves 8

### NUT PASTRY
- ☐ **¹/3 cup (50 g) finely chopped hazelnuts (filberts)**
- ☐ **1 teaspoon mixed spice**
- ☐ **ingredients for 1 recipe Rich Shortcrust Pastry**
- ☐ **vanilla extract**

### APPLE AND DATE FILLING
- ☐ **4 apples, peeled, cored and quartered**
- ☐ **6 tablespoons (90 g) butter**
- ☐ **³/4 cup (100 g) fresh dates, chopped**
- ☐ **¹/2 teaspoon cinnamon**
- ☐ **¹/2 cup (125 g) firmly packed brown sugar**
- ☐ **¹/2 cup (125 mL) honey**
- ☐ **¹/2 cup (125 mL) water**
- ☐ **¹/2 teaspoon vanilla extract**
- ☐ **¹/2 cup (60 g) all-purpose flour**
- ☐ **1 egg, lightly beaten**

1  To prepare pastry, combine hazelnuts and spice with flour and add a few drops vanilla to the egg yolk. Make as directed in the basic recipe. Roll out pastry on a lightly floured surface and line a lightly greased deep 9-inch (23 cm) tart pan. Allow to rest in the refrigerator for 15 minutes. Place on a cookie sheet and blind bake at 425°F (220°C) for 10 minutes. Remove beans and paper and cook for 10 minutes longer.
2  To make filling, cut each apple quarter into four slices. Melt 4 tablespoons (50 g) of butter in a skillet and cook apples for 3-4 minutes. Remove from skillet and arrange evenly over pastry shell. Sprinkle with dates and cinnamon.
3  Place sugar, honey, water, remaining butter and vanilla in a saucepan and cook over a medium heat until sugar has dissolved. Bring to the boil and simmer for 2 minutes.
4  Remove from heat and allow to cool for 15 minutes. Beat in flour and egg. Pour over apples and bake at 350°F (180°C) for 40-45 minutes or until filling is set. Serve hot or cold.

## APPLE AND LEMON TARTLETS

Makes 24

### SWEET PASTRY SHELLS
- ☐ **3 tablespoons superfine sugar**
- ☐ **vanilla extract**
- ☐ **ingredients for 1 recipe Rich Shortcrust Pastry**
- ☐ **3 tablespoons ground almonds**

## FILLING

- [ ] **4 cooking apples, peeled, cored and chopped**
- [ ] **2 tablespoons grated lemon rind**
- [ ] **3 tablespoons water**
- [ ] **1 teaspoon cinnamon**
- [ ] **5 tablespoons lemon juice**
- [ ] **1 cup (250 g) granulated sugar**
- [ ] **4 eggs, lightly beaten**
- [ ] **$^{1}/_{2}$ cup (1 stick/125 g) butter, chopped**

1   To prepare pastry shells, add sugar to flour and a few drops vanilla extract to egg yolk. Continue as directed in basic recipe. Roll out pastry on a lightly floured surface and sprinkle with ground almonds. Cut out rounds, using a 2$^{1}/_{2}$-inch (6 cm) pastry cutter, and place in greased tartlet pans. Prick bottoms with a fork and place them in refrigerator for 15 minutes. Bake at 400°F (200°C) for 15-20 minutes or until golden brown. Remove from oven and cool on a wire rack.

2   To make filling, place apples, lemon rind, water and cinnamon in a saucepan, bring to the boil and simmer for 15-20 minutes, or until reduced to a pulp. Place in a food processor or blender and process until smooth.

3   Transfer apple mixture to the top of a double saucepan. Add lemon juice and sugar and heat gently, stirring constantly, until sugar dissolves.

4   Remove from heat, gradually stir in the eggs and then the butter. Return to a very low heat and cook, stirring constantly, until the mixture becomes thick and creamy. Remove from heat and set aside to cool. Shortly before serving, spoon filling into pastry shells.

❖

## CREAMY CHICKEN PIE

Serves 6

### CHEESE PASTRY

- [ ] **$^{1}/_{2}$ cup (60 g) shredded Cheddar cheese**
- [ ] **1 teaspoon dry mustard**
- [ ] **$^{1}/_{2}$ teaspoon cayenne pepper**
- [ ] **ingredients for $^{1}/_{2}$ recipe Rich Shortcrust Pastry**

### CHICKEN FILLING

- [ ] **1 tablespoon olive oil**
- [ ] **1$^{1}/_{2}$ pounds (750 g) boned, skinned chicken breast halves, chopped**
- [ ] **$^{1}/_{4}$ cup ($^{1}/_{2}$ stick/60 g) butter**
- [ ] **1 clove garlic, crushed**
- [ ] **1 stalk celery, chopped**
- [ ] **1 onion, chopped**
- [ ] **3 tablespoons all-purpose flour**
- [ ] **1 cup (250 mL) chicken broth**
- [ ] **1 cup (250 mL) milk**

- [ ] **1 tablespoon chopped fresh parsley**
- [ ] **1 tablespoon chopped fresh rosemary**
- [ ] **freshly ground black pepper**

1   To prepare pastry, combine cheese, mustard and cayenne pepper and mix into flour. Continue as directed in basic recipe. Place in refrigerator to chill.

2   To make filling, heat oil in a large skillet and cook one-third of the chicken over a high heat for 3 minutes, or until cooked through. Remove from pan and repeat with remaining chicken.

3   Melt butter in skillet, add garlic, celery and onion and cook for 3-4 minutes, or until onion softens. Stir in flour and cook for 2 minutes longer. Remove pan from heat and stir in broth and milk. Return to heat, bring to the boil, stirring constantly, and simmer for 3 minutes. Add chicken, parsley and rosemary. Season to taste with pepper and set aside to cool.

4   Place filling into a pie dish. Roll out pastry to $^{1}/_{4}$-inch (5 mm) in thickness. Brush rim of pie dish with a little water and place the pastry over the filling. Trim edge with a knife and decorate as desired. Brush with a little milk and bake at 400°F (200°C) for 30-35 minutes or until golden brown.

### PASTRY-MAKING TIPS

✧ Place your utensils in the refrigerator to chill for 15-20 minutes before making pastry.

✧ The best pastry is made using chilled butter and water.

✧ Handle the pastry as little as possible.

✧ When you roll out the pastry roll away from you, lifting and turning to ensure an even thickness.

✧ Take care that you do not stretch the pastry when you are rolling it out.

✧ Rest the pastry in the refrigerator for 30 minutes before baking, to minimize shrinkage during cooking.

✧ Cook pastry in a 425°F (220°C) preheated oven.

✧ To make pastry in the food processor, place flour and butter in food processor and process to cut butter. Add egg yolk and water and process until dough is formed. Knead lightly and allow to rest before rolling.

*Creamy Chicken Pie*

# Easy desserts

By eliminating a long and laborious preparation, you need not eliminate variety and great taste. The following easy desserts will be sure to satisfy any discerning diner and will always end the meal perfectly.

## ❖
## APPLE ALMOND TARTS

Serves 4

- ☐ **12 oz (375 g) prepared short pastry**
- ☐ **1 cup (250 mL) canned apple sauce**
- ☐ **2 egg yolks, lightly beaten**
- ☐ **2 tablespoons honey**
- ☐ **3 tablespoons ground almonds**
- ☐ **3 tablespoons ground nutmeg**
- ☐ **2 large green apples, peeled, cored and finely sliced**
- ☐ **3 tablespoons lime marmalade, warmed**

1　Line four 4-inch (10 cm) tart pans with pastry. Line pastry shells with nonstick baking paper, fill with uncooked rice and bake at 375°F (190°C) for 10 minutes. Remove rice and paper and set aside to cool.
2　Place apple sauce, egg yolks, honey, almonds and nutmeg in a bowl and mix well. Spoon apple mixture into pastry shells and arrange apple slices over top.
3　Reduce oven temperature to 350°F (180°C) and bake for 20 minutes or until cooked through. Brush with melted marmalade. Serve hot, warm or cold with whipped cream.

## ❖
## ORANGE AND LEMON DELICIOUS PUDDING

*One of those magic puddings – as the pudding cooks it separates to give a layer of fluffy sponge over a tangy citrus sauce.*

Serves 6

- ☐ **1 cup (220 g) superfine sugar**
- ☐ **1/2 cup (1 stick/125 g) butter, softened**
- ☐ **1/2 cup (60 g) self-raising flour**
- ☐ **1 tablespoon finely grated lemon rind**
- ☐ **1 tablespoon finely grated orange rind**
- ☐ **2 tablespoons lemon juice**
- ☐ **2 tablespoons orange juice**
- ☐ **2 eggs, separated**
- ☐ **1 cup (250 mL) milk**

1　Place sugar and butter in a bowl and beat until light and fluffy. Mix in flour, lemon rind, orange rind, lemon juice and orange juice.
2　Place egg yolks and milk in a small bowl and whisk to combine. Mix into citrus mixture.
3　Beat egg whites until stiff peaks form then fold into batter. Spoon into a greased 4 cup (1 litre) capacity ovenproof dish. Place dish in a roasting pan with enough boiling water to come halfway up the sides of dish. Bake at 350°F (180°C) for 45 minutes or until cooked. Serve hot with cream or ice cream.

## ❖
## ORANGE FRENCH TOAST

Serves 4

- ☐ **3 eggs**
- ☐ **3 tablespoons milk**
- ☐ **2 tablespoons thick cream**
- ☐ **2 teaspoons vanilla extract**
- ☐ **2 tablespoons orange juice**
- ☐ **1 tablespoon grated orange rind**
- ☐ **1 plain or madeira loaf cake, cut into 1/2-inch (1 cm) slices**
- ☐ **2 tablespoons (30 g) butter**
- ☐ **whipped cream to serve**

1　Place eggs, milk, cream and vanilla extract in a bowl and beat until frothy. Stir in orange juice and orange rind.
2　Dip cake slices into egg mixture. Melt butter in a large skillet over a medium heat and cook cake slices for 2-3 minutes each side or until golden. Serve with whipped cream.

## ❖
## CUSTARD TART

Serves 8

- ☐ **1/2 cup (125 g) sugar**
- ☐ **3/4 cup (185 mL) water**
- ☐ **3 eggs**
- ☐ **3 tablespoons milk**
- ☐ **1 x 9-inch (23 cm) prepared sweet shortcrust pastry shell**
- ☐ **ground nutmeg**

1　Combine sugar and water in a saucepan and cook over a low heat, stirring constantly, for 4-5 minutes or until sugar dissolves. Set aside and allow to cool.
2　Place sugar syrup, eggs and milk in a mixing bowl and stir until combined. Pour into pastry shell and bake at 375°F (190°C) for 10 minutes. Reduce heat to 350°F (180°C) and bake for 20 minutes longer or until custard is firm. Serve hot, warm or cold sprinkled with nutmeg.

*Orange and Lemon Delicious Pudding*

# Take a custard

Custard is a favorite accompaniment to desserts and stewed fruits. It also forms the basis of many desserts.

## STIRRED CUSTARD

Makes 1 1/2 cups (375 mL)

- ☐ 3/4 **cup (190 mL) milk, scalded**
- ☐ **1 tablespoon sugar**
- ☐ **3 eggs, lightly beaten**
- ☐ 3/4 **cup (190 mL) cream**
- ☐ 1/2 **teaspoon vanilla**

1   Combine milk and sugar in a small saucepan and heat gently until sugar has dissolved.

2   Place eggs in top of a double boiler. Gradually stir in milk, then cream. Heat over simmering water, stirring constantly, until custard evenly coats the back of a wooden spoon.

3   Remove from heat and place top section of saucepan in iced water to stop the cooking process. Stir in vanilla and use custard as desired.

❖

## CREME ANGLAISE

*Crème Anglaise is a light custard sauce which is great served warm or chilled with fruit desserts and puddings.*

Makes 1 cup (250 mL)

- ☐ **3 egg yolks**
- ☐ 1 1/2 **tablespoons sugar**
- ☐ 1 1/4 **cups (300 mL) milk, scalded**
- ☐ 1/2 **teaspoon vanilla extract**

1   Combine egg yolks and sugar in a bowl. Place over a saucepan of simmering water and beat until a ribbon trail forms.

2   Gradually add milk and vanilla, stirring constantly. Transfer to a heavy-based saucepan and cook custard over a low heat, stirring in a figure-eight pattern, until it thickens and coats the back of a wooden spoon. Do not allow the custard to boil.

3   Remove pan from heat and place in a bowl of ice. Stir until custard cools a little. Strain through a fine sieve if necessary.

---

### SOUFFLE-MAKING TIPS

✧ Make preparing the dish and heating the oven your first steps.

✧ A soufflé will rise more evenly if it is placed on a cookie sheet to cook.

✧ Stir in 2-3 spoonfuls of beaten egg whites first, then fold in the remaining beaten whites. This lightens the mixture and the whites are more easily accepted by it.

✧ The soufflé will collapse if you open the oven door during cooking.

## NUT BAVARIAN CREAM

*These creamy surprises are laced with a hazelnut (filbert) praline, a delight to end any special meal. In this recipe the cream is served in chocolate cases, but if you wish they can be placed in small individual molds.*

Serves 10

- [ ] **4 tablespoons water**
- [ ] **1 cup (250 g) sugar**
- [ ] **3/4 cup (125 g) hazelnuts (filberts), toasted**
- [ ] **1 cup (250 mL) heavy cream, whipped**
- [ ] **1 tablespoon gelatin, dissolved in 3 tablespoons boiling water and cooled**
- [ ] **1 recipe Crème Anglaise, cooled**
- [ ] **10 chocolate cases (page 70)**

1  Place water and sugar in a small saucepan and stir over a medium heat until sugar dissolves. Brush down side of pan with a wet pastry brush. Bring to the boil and cook for 5-7 minutes, or until the toffee mixture turns golden brown.
2  Place nuts on a greased cookie sheet, pour toffee over. When cool, break apart and place in a food processor or blender and process. Fold whipped cream through.
3  Stir gelatin mixture into Crème Anglaise. Place over ice to become cold, stirring occasionally.
4  Fold the cream mixture through the Crème Anglaise as it begins to set. Spoon cream mixture into chocolate cases and refrigerate until set.

## INDIVIDUAL APRICOT TRIFLES

Serves 4

- [ ] **7-inch (18 cm) round sponge or butter cake, sliced**
- [ ] **1/2 cup (125 g) apricot jam**
- [ ] **14 oz (440 g) canned apricots, drained and sliced**
- [ ] **1 tablespoon ground nutmeg**
- [ ] **3 tablespoons apricot nectar**
- [ ] **3 tablespoons brandy**
- [ ] **1 recipe (375 mL) Stirred Custard**

1  Spread cake with jam. Place half the cake in the bottom of four individual glass dessert dishes, top with half the apricots and sprinkle with a little nutmeg. Repeat layers with remaining cake, apricots and nutmeg.
2  Divide apricot nectar, brandy and custard into four portions and pour over cake and apricots. Cover and refrigerate until ready to serve.

## LAYERED STRAWBERRY SOUFFLE

Serves 6

- [ ] **2 tablespoons Amaretto almond liqueur**
- [ ] **2 tablespoons Grand Marnier**
- [ ] **1 pint (250 g) strawberries, hulled and sliced**
- [ ] **4 egg yolks**
- [ ] **1/2 cup (85 g) superfine sugar**
- [ ] **4 tablespoons all-purpose flour**
- [ ] **1 1/4 cups (300 mL) milk, scalded**
- [ ] **1/2 teaspoon vanilla extract**
- [ ] **5 egg whites**

1  Combine Amaretto and Grand Marnier, add strawberries and set aside to macerate for 30 minutes.
2  Beat egg yolks and sugar until thick and light, then fold in flour. Combine milk and vanilla and whisk into egg mixture.
3  Transfer to a saucepan and heat gently, stirring until sauce boils and thickens. Reduce heat and simmer for 2 minutes.
4  Beat egg whites until stiff peaks form. Fold quickly and lightly through sauce, using a metal spoon. Place half the strawberries in the base of a lightly greased 8-inch (20 cm) soufflé dish with collar attached and pour over half the soufflé mixture. Repeat with remaining fruit and mixture.
5  Bake at 350°F (180°C) for 25-30 minutes, or until well risen and golden brown.

### SOUFFLE COLLARS

To make a soufflé collar, cut a piece of greaseproof paper 2 inches (5 cm) longer than the circumference of the soufflé dish. Fold in half lengthwise to give a double thickness. Brush with melted butter and sprinkle with dry bread crumbs, for a savory soufflé, or superfine sugar for a sweet soufflé. Wrap the paper collar around the soufflé dish. The soufflé dish should also be greased and sprinkled with bread crumbs or sugar; the collar should extend about 2 inches (5 cm) above the rim of the dish. Tie in place with string.

*Left: Nut Bavarian Cream, Individual Apricot Trifles*
*Above: Layered Strawberry Soufflé*

# Take some fruit

Fruit makes a wonderful dessert served on its own or try one of the delicious fruit desserts below.

❖
## FRUIT PLATTER WITH CREAMY APRICOT SAUCE

Serves 4

- ☐ $3/4$ cup (150 g) dried apricot halves
- ☐ 1 cup (250 mL) boiling water
- ☐ $1^1/2$ cups (375 g) sour cream or plain yogurt
- ☐ 2 tablespoons brown sugar
- ☐ 1 tablespoon dark rum
- ☐ selection of fruit, prepared and arranged on a platter

1   Soak apricots in water for 1 hour. Place in a food processor or blender and process until smooth.
2   Combine purée, sour cream, brown sugar and rum in a bowl and mix well. Serve with fruit as a dipping sauce.

---

### COOK'S TIP

Sauce may be made a day ahead and kept covered in the refrigerator.
✧   If you would like to serve the sauce hot, heat gently over a low heat in a small saucepan. Take care not to allow the sauce to boil.

---

### GELATIN TIPS

✧   To dissolve gelatin pour hot liquid into a container, sprinkle gelatin over and whisk with a fork until dissolved.
✧   The microwave oven is great for dissolving gelatin; mix the gelatin with cold water and cook on HIGH (100%) power for 45 seconds.
✧   In warm weather you may need to increase the gelatin quantity by half to insure setting.
✧   Insure that the gelatin mixture is the same temperature as the mixture to which it is to be added. If the two are at different temperatures tough strands form and separation occurs.

---

❖❖
## INDIVIDUAL FRUIT POTS

*Quick and easy, these fruit jellies make a delicious dessert.*

Serves 6

- ☐ $3/4$ cup (150 g) canned apricot halves, drained
- ☐ $1/2$ pint (150 g) strawberries, hulled and quartered
- ☐ 7 oz (200 g) black grapes
- ☐ 1 orange, segmented
- ☐ 2 tablespoons brandy
- ☐ 3 oz (90 g) package lemon gelatin
- ☐ $1^3/4$ cups (450 mL) boiling water

1   Soak apricots, strawberries, grapes and orange in brandy for 30 minutes.
2   Dissolve jelly crystals in water, set aside and allow to cool to room temperature.
3   Place half the fruit in six, moistened individual molds. Cover with half the jelly, place in the refrigerator and allow to set. Top with remaining fruit and jelly and return to refrigerator until set.

---

❖
## FRUIT CREPES WITH LEMON CREAM

*In this recipe, the crêpes are filled with a sweet filling, however the same recipe can be used for savory crêpes.*

Serves 4

- ☐ $1/2$ pint (150 g) papaya, cut into pieces
- ☐ $1/2$ pint (150 g) strawberries, hulled and quartered
- ☐ 2 tamarillos, peeled and cut into pieces
- ☐ 2 pears, peeled, cored and cut into pieces
- ☐ 3 tablespoons Cointreau
- ☐ $1/2$ cup (125 mL) water
- ☐ $1/2$ cup (125 g) sugar

CREPES
- ☐ $3/4$ cup (185 g) all-purpose flour, sifted
- ☐ $1/2$ cup (125 mL) water
- ☐ $1/2$ cup (125 mL) milk
- ☐ 2 eggs
- ☐ butter for cooking

LEMON CREAM
- ☐ 3 tablespoons lemon juice
- ☐ $3/4$ cup (190 mL) thick cream
- ☐ 2 teaspoons confectioners' sugar
- ☐ 2 teaspoons chopped fresh mint

1   Place papaya, strawberries, tamarillos and pears in a bowl. Pour Cointreau over, cover and refrigerate overnight.
2   Place water and sugar in a small saucepan and cook over a medium heat until sugar dissolves. Occasionally brush down the side with a moistened pastry brush. Bring to the boil and simmer for 5 minutes. Remove from heat and set aside to cool. Pour over fruit and chill.
3   To make crêpes, combine flour, water, milk and eggs in a large bowl. Mix until smooth. Melt butter in a crêpe pan and pour in 2 tablespoons mixture. Cook for 1 minute on each side or until pale golden.
4   To make cream, beat together lemon juice, cream and confectioners' sugar. Fold mint through.
5   To serve, place fruit in the center of crêpes and roll up. Place on serving plate and top with Lemon Cream.

*Fruit Crêpes with Lemon Cream, Fruit Platter with Creamy Apricot Sauce, Individual Fruit Pots*

# Take a cake
## ...And Make A Dessert

The following desserts are all made using the Basic Butter Cake on page 74. From this one recipe you can make steamed and self-saucing puddings as well as cakes.

## SELF-SAUCING BROWNIE PUDDING

Serves 8

- ☐ **1 recipe Basic Chocolate Cake mixture (page 74)**
- ☐ **2 tablespoons cocoa**
- ☐ **¹/2 cup (85 g) packed brown sugar**
- ☐ **1¹/2 cups (375 mL) boiling water**
- ☐ **confectioners' sugar**

1   Place cake mixture in a greased 8-cup (2 litre) ovenproof dish. Sift cocoa and sugar over mixture. Carefully pour water evenly over top and bake at 350°F (180°C) for 40 minutes or until pudding is firm. Stand 10 minutes before serving. To serve, dust lightly with confectioners' sugar.

### COOK'S TIP
If your pudding mold does not have a fitted lid, tie a double thickness of foil over the mold with string.

## GOLDEN STEAMED PUDDING

Serves 8

- ☐ **5 tablespoons honey**
- ☐ **1 recipe Basic Butter Cake mixture (page 74)**

1   Spread honey over the bottom of a greased 6-cup (1.5 litre) pudding mold. Pour cake mixture over honey. Cover with a round of greased paper, then a round of foil and secure with pudding mold lid.
2   Place mold in a large saucepan with enough boiling water to come halfway up the side of the basin. Steam for 1¹/2 hours, or until pudding is cooked through; replace water as the pudding cooks. Allow to stand for 5 minutes before turning out.

## STEAMED FRUIT PUDDING WITH BRANDY CREAM

Serves 8

- ☐ **¹/2 cup (90 g) golden raisins**
- ☐ **¹/2 cup (75 g) currants**
- ☐ **¹/2 cup (80 g) dates, chopped**
- ☐ **1 teaspoon ground cinnamon**
- ☐ **1 teaspoon ground mixed spice**
- ☐ **1 quantity Basic Butter Cake mixture (page 74)**

BRANDY CREAM
- ☐ **¹/2 cup (125 mL) sour cream**
- ☐ **¹/2 cup (125 mL) thickened cream**
- ☐ **1 tablespoon brown sugar**
- ☐ **1 tablespoon brandy**

1   Combine raisins, currants, dates, cinnamon and mixed spice and fold through cake mixture.
2   Pour batter into a greased 6-cup (1.5 litre) pudding mold. Cover with a round of lightly greased paper, then foil and pudding mold lid.
3   Place mold in a large saucepan with enough boiling water to come halfway up the side of the basin. Boil for 1 hour or until pudding is firm, replacing water if necessary as the pudding cooks. Allow to stand for 5 minutes before turning out.
4   To make cream, combine sour cream, cream, brown sugar and brandy in a bowl and mix well. Serve with hot pudding.

### Variation
**Spicy Ginger Pudding:** Add ¹/2 teaspoon of ground ginger and ¹/2 teaspoon of mixed spice to the flour when making the Basic Butter Cake mixture. Replace the fruit with 1 cup (100 g) chopped preserved ginger in syrup.

# Take a cheesecake

Left: Steamed Fruit Pudding with
Brandy Cream, Self-Saucing Brownie
Pudding, Golden Pudding
Above: Creamy Cheese Hearts with
Mango Sauce, Mini Cheesecakes in
Pastry (page 89)

## CREAMY CHEESE HEARTS WITH MANGO SAUCE

Serves 8

- ☐ ¹/₂ cup (125 g) dried mango, chopped
- ☐ 2 tablespoons brandy
- ☐ 1 recipe Basic Cheesecake filling, cream cheese omitted
- ☐ 1 cup (250 g) mascarpone cheese

SAUCE

- ☐ 3 mangoes, peeled and chopped
- ☐ 1 tablespoon superfine sugar
- ☐ 2 tablespoons fresh orange juice
- ☐ 2 teaspoons Grand Marnier

1   Place mango and brandy in a small bowl and set aside to macerate for 1-2 hours. Make up the cheesecake mixture as in the basic recipe, replacing the cream cheese with mascarpone. Fold through dried mango and brandy.

2   Pour into greased and lined individual coeur à la crème molds and bake at 250°F (120°C) for 55-60 minutes or until just firm. Turn oven off and cool molds in oven with door ajar. Refrigerate for several hours. Turn out.

3   To make sauce, place mangoes, superfine sugar, orange juice and Grand Marnier in a food processor or blender and process until smooth. Serve with cheese hearts.

### COOK'S TIP

✧  Molds of any shape can be used to make the Creamy Cheese Hearts.

✧  Mascarpone cheese is an Italian dessert cheese that can be purchased from cheese shops and some supermarkets.

✧  The fresh and dried mango used in the Creamy Cheese Hearts can be replaced with dried, fresh or canned apricots or peaches.

❖

## BASIC CHEESECAKE

Serves 8

### BASE
- ☐ 1$^1$/$_2$ cups (200 g) plain sweet cookie crumbs
- ☐ $^1$/$_2$ cup (1 stick/125 g) butter, melted
- ☐ 1 teaspoon mixed spice
- ☐ $^1$/$_2$ teaspoon ground ginger

### FILLING
- ☐ 1 cup (250 g) cream cheese
- ☐ 1 cup (250 g) ricotta cheese
- ☐ $^2$/$_3$ cup (170 g) superfine sugar
- ☐ 3 eggs
- ☐ 3 tablespoons all-purpose flour, sifted
- ☐ 1 tablespoon lemon juice
- ☐ 1 teaspoon vanilla extract
- ☐ $^3$/$_4$ cup (190 mL) thick cream

1  To make crust, combine cookie crumbs, butter, mixed spice and ginger in a bowl and mix well. Press over the bottom and side of a greased 8-inch (20 cm) springform pan. Refrigerate until firm.

2  To make filling, beat cream cheese, ricotta and sugar until sugar dissolves. Add eggs one at a time, beating well after each addition. Fold through flour and then lemon juice, vanilla and cream.

3  Pour mixture into prepared crust and bake at 250°F (120°C) for 1$^1$/$_2$ hours or until just firm in the center. Turn oven off and cool cheesecake in oven with door ajar. Refrigerate for several hours, or overnight before serving.

## Variations

**Double Chocolate and Pecan Cheesecake:** Make the crust using plain sweet chocolate cookies. Omit mixed spice and ginger. Omit the lemon juice from the filling and fold 5 oz (150 g) melted dark chocolate and $^3$/$_4$ cup (100 g) chopped pecans through with the cream. Continue as directed in the basic recipe.

**Ginger Honey Cheesecake:** Omit mixed spice and add 1 extra tablespoon ground ginger to the crust. In the filling, replace 3 tablespoons superfine sugar with 3 tablespoons of honey. Toss 1 cup (100 g) finely chopped glacé ginger or preserved ginger in syrup, drained, in a little flour and fold through the filling. Continue as for the basic recipe.

**Strawberry Cheesecake:** Arrange 1 pint (250 g) of hulled and quartered strawberries over the cookie crust. Continue as for the basic recipe.

## COOK'S TIP

✧ You may wish to replace the cookie crust of the cheesecakes with the sweet shortcrust pastry used for the Apple and Lemon Tartlets on page 78.

✧ When preparing the pan for the cheesecake turn the base upside down and cover with foil. This will make the bottom much easier to remove.

❖

## MINI CHEESECAKES
## IN PASTRY

*These mini cheesecakes surrounded in filo pastry are a perfect finish to any dinner party and may be served hot or cold.*

Serves 6

- ☐ **5 tablespoons golden raisins**
- ☐ **2 tablespoons chopped dried apricots**
- ☐ **1 teaspoon ground cinnamon**
- ☐ **$^1/_2$ recipe Basic Cheesecake filling**
- ☐ **6 sheets filo pastry**
- ☐ **$^1/_4$ cup ($^1/_2$ stick/50 g) butter, melted**

1 Combine raisins, apricots and cinnamon and fold through cheesecake mixture.

2 Place pastry sheets on top of one another and cut into six square sections. Taking six individual squares, brush each pastry sheet with butter and place another sheet on top at a different angle. Repeat with remaining four squares. Repeat with remaining pastry and butter. Line greased muffin pans with pastry and fill with cheesecake mixture.

3 Bake at 350°F (180°C) for 20-25 minutes, or until mixture is cooked through and pastry is golden brown.

*Left: Basic Cheesecake, Double Chocolate and Pecan Cheesecake*
*Right: Ginger Honey Cheesecake, Strawberry Cheesecake*

Glass Cake Stands from HAG

# Glossary of cooking terms and techniques

**Al dente:** Just firm to the bite, the correct texture for pasta, rice and some vegetables.

**Au gratin:** A cheese and bread crumb topping, browned under the broiler or in the oven.

**Bind:** To hold dry ingredients together with egg or liquid.

**Blind baking:** To bake blind, line the pastry with a sheet of baking paper or aluminum foil. Weigh it down with dried beans, uncooked rice or pasta. The quantity should be enough to compensate for the filling and be pushed well out to the edges so that the sides are supported. Bake the pastry shell at 400°F (200°C) for 10 minutes or as directed in the recipe. Remove lining and beans and bake pastry shell for 7-10 minutes longer or until pastry is cooked through and lightly browned. Cool pastry shell before filling. Allow beans, rice or pasta to cool completely, then store in an airtight container for future use. Do not use for any other purpose.

*Line pastry shell with paper and weigh down with beans, rice or pasta*

**Bouillon:** Broth or uncleared stock.

**Bouquet garni:** A small bunch of herbs, usually parsley, thyme and bay leaf. A bouquet garni is added to stews, soups or stocks for flavoring. Commercially prepared sachets of dried herbs are also available at most supermarkets.

## CHICKEN

### To section a chicken:

1  Using a sharp knife, cut through skin where the leg joins the body, then cut through the bone joint between the leg and the body. This section consists of the leg and thigh and is called a Maryland. Separate thigh from the leg by cutting through the joint.

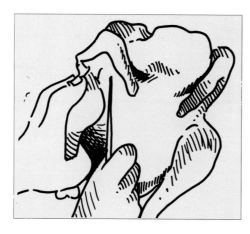

2  Cut a small amount of breast meat down through the wing section, bending wing away from body to reveal joint. Cut through joint bone.

3  Cut through rib bones, along each side of the body between breast and back to separate the two pieces. The back portion can be frozen and used at a later date for the stock pot.

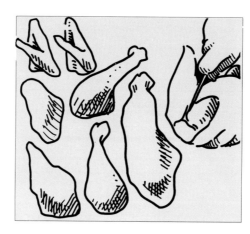

4  Divide the breast section into two pieces by cutting through the center of the breast bone. Trim all pieces of excess fat and skin.

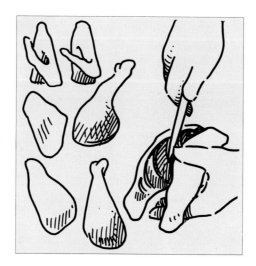

**Trussing a chicken:** Trussing a chicken helps it maintain its shape during cooking. Insert a metal skewer crosswise, just below the thigh bone, right through the body of the chicken. The ends of the skewer should be exposed either side. Place the chicken breast side down on a work surface. Take a length of string and catch in wing tips, then pass string under ends of skewer and cross over the back. Turn the chicken breast side up and tie in legs and the "parson's nose".

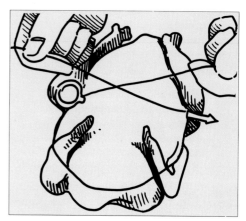

*Place chicken breast side down then pass string under ends of skewer then cross over the back*

**Clarify:** To melt and strain butter of its milk particles and impurities. Also means to clear stocks and jellies by filtering.

**Consommé:** Concentrated clear meat or poultry stock.

## EGGS

**Separating eggs:** To separate an egg, crack the shell by tapping with the back of a knife to break cleanly in half. Carefully pass the yolk from one half of the shell to the other, so that the white of the egg passes into a bowl. Then place the yolk in a separate bowl. If separating more than one egg, break into separate bowls to ensure freshness before adding to the other eggs. If egg white is to be beaten to soft or stiff peak stage, it is vital that not a speck of yolk goes into white, as the white will not beat up.

**Beating egg whites:** To beat egg whites, to "soft peaks" or "firm peaks" requires a little care. Firstly, all utensils being used must be free of grease and very clean. The smallest amount of grease, or even the smallest amount of egg yolk, will spoil the end result. If the whites are overbeaten, they become difficult to fold through and the mixture could collapse when cooking.
**Soft peaks:** Form in round mounds after beating for a short time at a high speed, if using an electric mixer.

**Firm peaks:** Slightly dryer and more peaked in shape than soft peaks. Use beaten egg whites immediately; if left to stand they will collapse.

**Flake:** To separate cooked fish flesh into small pieces.
**Fold in:** To combine two mixtures gently with a large metal spoon or spatula still retaining lightness.

GARNISHES

**Chili tulips:** Cut three-quarters down the length of chili, using sharp scissors. Remove seeds, then cut down each three times. Put chili in a bowl of iced water. Refrigerate until chili opens and curls.

**Green onion curls:** Cut the bulb from the onion just where it starts to turn green. Trim the tops to give a total length of 4 inches (10 cm). Using sharp scissors, cut down each green top to the hard stem; repeat eight times. Put onions in a bowl of iced water. Refrigerate for about 20-30 minutes or until onion curls. Simple curls can be made by cutting thin strips of the green part of the onion. Place in iced water, as for curls, until just curled.

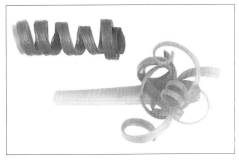

**Lemon and lime twists:** Cut thin slices of lemon or lime, then cut each slice through to the center. Twist the two bottom halves in opposite directions and place in position.

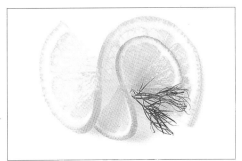

**Celery curls:** Cut washed celery stalks into 2-inch (5 cm) lengths, then using the point of a sharp knife cut down the length in narrow widths, almost to the base. Put the celery in a bowl of iced water and refrigerate until curled.
**Hull:** To remove green stem from fruit.

**Leeks:** To prepare and clean, cut down lengthwise and dunk upside down in a bowl of cold water to remove dirt.

*Cleaning leeks*

**Lettuce:** To wash and separate the lettuce leaves, remove the stem of the lettuce using a twisting motion with hand until stem comes free. For firmer, tighter stems, cut free from lettuce using the point of a sharp knife. Place lettuce, stem side up, under cold running water. The weight of the continually running water will cause the leaves to separate. For crisp leaves, shake off excess water and place in a plastic freezer bag, tie and refrigerate for 30 minutes, or until required.
**Measuring up:** As you progress with your cooking techniques, you will gradually acquire equipment. However, for sucessful results in cooking correct measuring is essential. Make a set of measuring cups, spoons and liquid measurement jugs number one priority on your list of kitchen equipment. To measure dry ingredients, shake loosely into the required cup; do not pack firmly unless directed otherwise. Level by drawing a spatula or knife across top of the cup. To measure liquids, pour in the required amount, place the jug on a flat surface and check at eye level.

*A set of measuring cups and spoons*

**Meat:** To roll and secure loin of meat, place stuffing along flap, roll loin up firmly and hold in position with skewers or poultry pins. Cut a long piece of string, place under the meat at one end, bringing the two ends – one long length, one short length – to the top of meat. Twist the ends and knot. Then, working with the long length of string, extend out along the top of meat 1 inch (2.5 cm), hold in position with finger at that point while passing the remaining length down the side, under and up the other side of meat. Loop under finger position and pull long length to tighten. Continue in this manner along the loin, knotting at the other end.

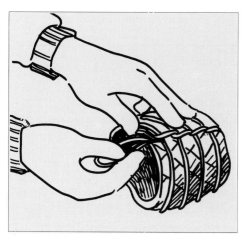

*Tie loin using strong string*

**Parboil (blanch):** To boil for part of the cooking time before finishing by another method.

PASTRY DECORATIONS
Put a professional finish to your pies with simple pastry decorations.
**Pastry leaves:** Cut leftover pastry scraps into 1-inch ( 2.5 cm) strips, then diagonally across to form diamond shapes. Mark with the back of a knife to resemble veins on leaves. Arrange decoratively in the center of glazed pie or overlap leaves and use as a decorative edging.
**To make a lattice pattern for pies:** Cut the pastry into $1/2$-inch (10 mm) wide strips, long enough to cover the pie. Moisten the edges with water and lay half the strips over the filling, about 1-inch (2.5 cm) apart. Then lay the remaining strips diagonally across these. Trim off excess and press edges together.
**Poach:** To cook by simmering very gently in liquid.
**Reduce:** To concentrate or thicken a liquid by rapid boiling.
**Refresh:** To rinse freshly cooked food in cold water to cease the cooking process and set the color, usually with green vegetables.

**Rest:** To allow the protein in flour (gluten) to contract after kneading and rolling pastry. To allow the starch cells in batter to expand, for example when making crêpes.
**Roux:** A blend of melted butter and flour, cooked as a base for thickening sauces and soups.
**Scald:** To heat liquid, usually milk, to just below boiling point.
**Sear:** To brown meat quickly on a hot surface to retain juices.
**Skim:** To remove scum or fat from the surface of a liquid.

VEGETABLE PREPARATION
**Cube:** Cut into about $1/2$-inch (1 cm) pieces.
**Dice:** Cut into $1/4$-inch (0.5 cm) pieces.
**Grind:** Cut into $1/8$-inch (0.25 cm) pieces.
**Shred:** Use either a hand grater or a food processor with a fine shredding attachment.
**Slice:** Cut either very thin to thick. You can also slice into rings. Another way to slice is to cut diagonally. This is a good way to prepare vegetables such as carrots, celery and zucchini for stir-frying.

**Toasting nuts and coconut:** Coconut can be toasted by spreading the required amount over a cookie sheet, then baking at 350°F (180°C) for 5-10 minutes, or until coconut is lightly and evenly browned. Toss back and forth occasionally with a spoon to ensure even browning. Nuts can be toasted in the same manner or placed on a tray and browned under the broiler on a medium heat. Toss back and forth with a spoon until lightly and evenly browned.

| Cubed | Diced | Minced | Shredded | Sliced |

# Useful information

*Glossary of ingredients*

**Best end neck chops:** Middle neck of lamb chops.

**Bread crumbs, soft:** 1- or 2-day-old bread made into crumbs.

**Bread crumbs, packaged:** Use commercially packaged bread crumbs.

**Canned baby corn:** If unavailable use fresh baby corn cobs, lightly blanched.

**Chili sauce:** A sauce which includes chilies, salt and vinegar.

**Coconut cream:** A thick coconut paste; if unavailable dissolve chopped creamed coconut in boiling water.

**Coconut milk:** Available canned or as a powder which is reconstituted by mixing with water. Coconut milk may also be made by dissolving 1/4 cup (50 g) creamed coconut in 5 ounces (150 mL) of boiling water.

**Cornflour:** Cornstarch.

**English spinach:** Summer spinach.

**Mignonette lettuce:** A round lettuce with reddish leaves, sometimes called Four Seasons or Quatro Stagioni.

**Muffin pans:** Deep tartlet tins.

**Pork butterfly steaks:** Thick pork steaks cut from the loin, then cut almost through horizontally and opened out to make a butterfly shape.

**Ready-rolled puff pastry:** If unavailable, roll out puff pastry and cut into size required.

**Snapper:** A tropical fish.

**Snow peas:** Mangetout.

**Sour cream:** Commercially soured cream

**Stock:** Homemade gives best results. For a convenient substitute use a commercially available broth preparation.

**Tomato paste:** Tomato purée.

In this book, ingredients such as fish and meat are given in pounds (grams) so you know how much to buy. A small inexpensive set of kitchen scales is always handy and very easy to use. Other ingredients in our recipes are given in tablespoons and cups, so you will need a nest of measuring cups (1 cup, 1/2 cup, 1/3 cup and 1/4 cup), a set of spoons (1 tablespoon, 1 teaspoon, 1/2 teaspoon and 1/4 teaspoon) and a transparent graduated measuring jug (1 quart and 1 cup) for measuring liquids. Cup and spoon measures are level.

## MEASURING UP

| Cups | Metric | Imperial |
|---|---|---|
| 1/4 cup | 60 mL | 2 fl oz |
| 1/3 cup | 80 mL | 2 1/2 fl oz |
| 1/2 cup | 125 mL | 4 fl oz |
| 1 cup | 250 mL | 8 fl oz |

### Metric Measuring Spoons

| | |
|---|---|
| 1/4 teaspoon | 1.25 mL |
| 1/2 teaspoon | 2.5 mL |
| 1 teaspoon | 5 mL |
| 1 tablespoon | 20 mL |

## MEASURING LIQUIDS

| Metric | Imperial | Cup |
|---|---|---|
| 30 mL | 1 fl oz | |
| 60 mL | 2 fl oz | 1/4 cup |
| 90 mL | 3 fl oz | |
| 125 mL | 4 fl oz | 1/2 cup |
| 170 mL | 5 1/2 fl oz | 2/3 cup |
| 185 mL | 6 fl oz | |
| 220 mL | 7 fl oz | |
| 250 mL | 8 fl oz | 1 cup |
| 500 mL | 16 fl oz | 2 cups |
| 600 mL | 1 pint | |

## MEASURING DRY INGREDIENTS

| Metric | Imperial |
|---|---|
| 15 g | 1/2 oz |
| 30 g | 1 oz |
| 60 g | 2 oz |
| 90 g | 3 oz |
| 125 g | 4 oz |
| 155 g | 5 oz |
| 185 g | 6 oz |
| 220 g | 7 oz |
| 250 g | 8 oz |
| 280 g | 9 oz |
| 315 g | 10 oz |
| 350 g | 11 oz |
| 375 g | 12 oz |
| 410 g | 13 oz |
| 440 g | 14 oz |
| 470 g | 15 oz |
| 500 g | 16 oz (1 lb) |
| 750 g | 1 lb 8 oz |
| 1 kg | 2 lb |
| 1.5 kg | 3 lb |
| 2 kg | 4 lb |
| 2.5 kg | 5 lb |

## QUICK CONVERTER

| Metric | Imperial |
|---|---|
| 5 mm | 1/4 in |
| 1 cm | 1/2 in |
| 2 cm | 3/4 in |
| 2.5 cm | 1 in |
| 5 cm | 2 in |
| 10 cm | 4 in |
| 15 cm | 6 in |
| 20 cm | 8 in |
| 23 cm | 9 in |
| 25 cm | 10 in |
| 30 cm | 12 in |

## OVEN TEMPERATURES

| °C | °F | Gas Mark |
|---|---|---|
| 120 | 250 | 1/2 |
| 140 | 275 | 1 |
| 150 | 300 | 2 |
| 160 | 325 | 3 |
| 180 | 350 | 4 |
| 190 | 375 | 5 |
| 200 | 400 | 6 |
| 220 | 425 | 7 |
| 240 | 475 | 8 |
| 250 | 500 | 9 |

# Index